I0493454

THE CROWDSOURCED

Guide to Freelancing

Collated by Daniel Hall

Copyright © 2014 Daniel Hall
All rights reserved.

THE CROWDSOURCED GUIDE TO FREELANCING

SERIES : CROWDSOURCED GUIDES

ISBN - 13: 978-1496158086 (Paperback edition)

Book Design & Layout by Andrea L. - eBookSmithy@gmail.com

No part of this publication may be reproduced, stored in a retrieval system, or transmitted in any form or by any means, mechanical, electronic, photocopying, recording, or otherwise, without the written permission of the publisher, except for brief quotations embedded in critical reviews and a number of other non-commercial uses permitted by copyright law. British English.

Preface

'The Crowdsourced Guide To Freelancing' is the second in a series of 'Crowdsourced Guides'. It follows on from the first book in the series titled 'The Crowdsourced Guide To Business'. I have collated these guides because over the past few years people have begun to see the value of crowdsourced information. Getting the views of several authors gives the reader a far more rounded view of a subject compared to a traditional information book where only one author passes on his knowledge. Not only do readers get more tips by reading the thoughts of several authors, but can also be more confident in the information they receive by looking out for recurring themes, whilst anomalies should be viewed with caution. With traditional guides, readers are not fortunate enough to have this filter from misinformation and biases.

The purpose of this particular book is to help people decide whether they should become freelancers or not. If the reader does decide they want to become a freelancer then they can also find tips on how to win work, where to find work and how to keep clients happy. It focuses on the experiences of a handful of successful freelancers. The particular freelancers who contributed to this book were chosen because they have flawless feedback and have each carried out a lot of jobs. This allows the contributors to give solid advice rather than seeking information from those who have not been able to win a lot of work on freelance work websites or those who have received unfavourable feedback from clients.

Whilst this book contains the perspectives of people who freelance within different industries, I have predominantly sought information from those who freelance as writers. The reason behind this is that all freelancers no matter what industry they work in, face the same problems. But people who write for a living were all likely to express this information in an understandable and compelling way for readers.

I choose freelancing as the subject for the second book in the series because I myself have freelanced for about a year and a half now, so I felt I could pass on some good advice. Freelancing is also becoming an extremely popular way for people to work. Following a study, it was estimated by the software company Intuit in 2010 that by 2020, 40% of Americans will work as freelancers.[1] Not only this but the number of registered freelancers on the website Elance more than doubled between the start of 2012 and the end of 2013. This was an increase of 2 million members, taking the total number of members on the site to 3.5 million members.[2] With more and more people becoming freelancers every day I hope that The Crowdsourced Guide To Freelancing can become a valuable resource to them.

I would like to take this opportunity to thank everyone who has contributed to the book.

[1] Quartz. "40% of America's workforce will be freelancers by 2020 – Quartz." Accessed February 18, 2014,
http://qz.com/65279/40-of-americas-workforce-will-be-freelancers-by-2020/
[2] "Global Online Employment Report Online Work Report on Jobs and Earnings Elance." Accessed February 18, 2014,
https://www.elance.com/q/online-employment-report

INTRODUCTION

Are you thinking about becoming a freelancer? Do you want to find out the positives and negatives of freelancing as a career? Do you want tips on how to successfully win work? And once you have won this work would you like to know how to accumulate perfect feedback and how to keep your clients happy? Then you must read this book.

All of the contributors to this book are successful freelancers who have a wealth of experience behind them. They were chosen especially due to the established reputations they hold on big freelancing websites and the cumulative knowledge that they can pass on to readers.

By reading this book you will be able to make an informed decision on whether to become a freelancer or not. If it is a path that you choose to pursue then you will skip months of 'on the job learning' and mistakes that most freelancers make when they first start out. The Crowdsourced Guide To Freelancing is your chance to get ahead of the game.

I have written this particular book because I am passionate about freelancing. I myself have been freelancing for just over a year and a half. During that time I have gone on to amass the best feedback on Elance for Pay Per Click services which has allowed me to be able to pick and choose which clients I work for. On a daily basis I have six or seven potential clients specifically ask me to run their accounts for them and if I bid on a job that I wasn't personally invited to, I usually go on to be awarded the job. As the freelance marketplace is growing every day I want to be able to pass this information on to the readers of this book so that you too can benefit from what freelancing has to offer.

Like 'The Crowdsourced Guide To Business' before it and all future 'Crowdsourced Guides', this book has been written without any padding. Each contribution starts by highlighting its author and then goes straight in to questions and answers. This allows the reader to get the information they want quickly, without the need to read tons of fluff first.

With the information contained in this book being so valuable and the format set out so that it is extremely easy to read there is no excuse not to read on.

CONTENTS

Freelancing

Caitlin White

https://www.goodreads.com/author/show/7164084.Caitlin_White

Caitlin has been a freelancer since mid-July 2013. She's been writing for nigh on ten years and is truly passionate about the craft. When she isn't writing, she's reading or running after her toddler. She enjoys longs walks on the beaches of her imagination, and specializes in articles, fiction short stories and full-length novels, ghost writing, editing, proofreading, social media management, WordPress, and general virtual assistant duties. She picked up all these skills by actively working with clients, and not by studying anything related to the field. She has an Honours degree in Behavioural Genetics.

1. What do you enjoy about being a freelancer?

The freedom. I have freedom of control over my clients, how much money I earn and the hours I work. As with anything in life, the harder you work, the more you earn. You really get to set your own boundaries rather than working for the 'man'. Also, if you work for someone who irritates you, you can choose to cut that relationship and move onto a job that sits better with you.

As a freelancer, you also govern your free time. I have a son (a two year old – help!) and he demands quite a lot of attention. I'm able to balance my work hours nicely and work from home. This way, he gets loads of attention and I make a tidy living.

2. What don't you enjoy about being a freelancer?

The glut of workers who don't value themselves. When you apply for jobs chances are there's going to be another freelancer who bids lower than you do. Their quality might not be anywhere near your standard, but they'll still get the job simply because they're asking for less. This is pretty much abhorrent. It really grates my cheese. I (and other freelancers out there) work exceptionally hard to deliver quality over quantity. I don't charge outrageous prices, but I don't undersell myself either. But there are plenty of freelancers that do undersell themselves, and they flood the 'market' with low prices which don't reflect the level of work that needs to be done for any given job.

The lesson? Don't sell yourself short.

3. Would you advise a friend to become a freelancer or would you advise they get a normal 9 to 5 job? And why?

I would advise a friend to become a freelancer IF they are willing to work just as hard as they would in a 9 to 5 job (perhaps even harder). You get flexible hours, sure, but you only earn as much effort as you put in. If you don't work, you don't earn and because there is just SO MUCH competition in the freelance writing market, it's likely you won't earn much at all. You have to start out at the bottom and work your butt off until you're confident enough to charge what you think you deserve.

However, there are lot of opportunities online. In the current economic climate it's becoming increasingly difficult to find a job in the area you studied in (Holla Behavioural Genetics!), and it's much easier to freelance and find work which matches your skills online.

4. What do you think is the best freelancing site and why?

It all depends on what you're looking to put out there. All freelancing sites have strict rules and take a cut of your cash at the end of the day. Freelancing sites are great jumping off points to meet new clients. For instance, I did articles for a client on Elance and that became a professional business relationship in another area (Social Media Management).

I would say Elance is just about the safest, and I'd advise freelancers to stick to the rules on these sites. Breaking them achieves nothing and takes the money out of your pocket. Fiverr is also a good site for those who have a specialized skill to market.

5. Have you ever picked up work outside of the freelance sites and if so how did you find this work?

Indeed I have. Check out Problogger.net for jobs listings outside of freelance sites. Setting up your own website is also a good way to attract business, as long as you couple it with some good SEO practices and a few social media accounts. Start with the freelancing sites and work your way up and off them, eventually you get paid more once you reach the higher levels.

6. Do you have any tips on how to win freelance jobs? (either on the freelance sites or outside of these).

Be professional but let your character shine through. Nobody likes boring, but nobody likes being greeted 'Yo, what's crackalackin', either. The same rules which apply in a live business interview, apply here. Short, sweet, professional and with character. Don't beg and don't ever bid with a stock letter.

For example:

Dear Sir,

I read your job posting thoroughly and believe I have the skills to fulfil… blablabla.

It's obvious that you didn't read the posting and you don't really care about anything other than the money. Clients don't like to feel like you're just after their cash, because that's an indication that you don't really care about what they want. And you should always care.

7. Do you have any tips on how to accumulate good feedback on the freelance sites?

Work hard and be efficient. Keep constant tabs on your account and answer messages swiftly. Always update your clients on the progress of the job, and be friendly and professional at all times. Deliver quality time and time again.

8. How do you keep your clients happy?

I deliver on time. I work hard. I'm loyal and friendly. I deliver QUALITY for money. I care. Common courtesy and hard work win the day every day. Going out of your way to make a client happy is also key. The harder you work and the more efficient you are, the more likely the client is to rehire you or think of you for another project in the future. Often, clients don't like to search the job market for every little task, so if they cotton on to someone who delivers quality work, they stick with them all the way through.

9. Do you have any tips on how to effectively manage your time?

This is one I struggle with a bit. I'm always overworking myself because I'm a bit too driven. I suggest you apply only to jobs you think you can complete within the set time period and that you don't set unreasonable time periods for yourself when applying. This will only lead to burnout and unhappy clients. Don't take on too much.

Create a calendar on your desktop or in Word and use it to track what is due when. Work methodically through your tasks and plan your hours at the beginning of each week. Remember to get enough sleep and food (and exercise!!!) or you'll end up missing deadlines and making a bad impression.

10. Do you prefer working by yourself or is freelancing a lonely life?

I love freelancing, but I don't really work by myself. I have clients that I communicate with via Skype for articles, virtual assistant duties, social media management and more. So, I'm not working by myself all the time. It can get a little bit lonely, but that's only if you live in a tiny town like I do. ;)

11. Do you have any other tips for people who want to be successful freelancers?

Get a PayPal account and set it up properly. Beware of scams! There are plenty of them out there. If a job offer says: 'You'll start low but get paid at least $400 per day', you know that it's a load o' plain hooey. Look out for yourself and draw up a contract services agreement which you'd be happy to sign – this way you have something to send or suggest to a client when starting new jobs. Be prepared to sign NDAs (Non-Disclosure Agreements) and practice patience – there are loads of people who are really vague on what they want and make you squish it out of them.

My Main Tip:

Build your portfolio before you hit the freelance market. Check out GKBCInc.com. They allow volunteers to join them and get your articles (and creative designs) published online. This helps you set up your writing resume and flesh it out. Clients are always on the lookout for online posts, rather than plain samples, so the more URLs you have (quality, of course) the better.

Christina DeBusk

http://cdebusk13.wordpress.com/

1. What do you enjoy about being a freelancer?

I would say that the thing I enjoy most about freelancing is being able to set my own schedule. I am a pretty self-disciplined person so I usually get up fairly early (anywhere from 3 – 6 AM) and get my work day done so that I can relax and enjoy life a little in the afternoon. However, if I want to sleep in, I can do that too and just work later. I'm flexible to work whatever shift suits me best on any given day.

Plus, the sky is the limit on my income as it's up to me how much I make (for the most part anyway). So, if I have a big expense coming up or want to tuck away some cash, for example, I have the ability to work more to meet those financial obligations and goals.

2. What don't you enjoy about being a freelancer?

I really miss having a steady paycheck. When I was in law enforcement and worked for the government, I knew I was going to get paid every two weeks as well as the minimum amount I would receive (overtime was always a bonus). Now, there is no such thing as overtime and the amount I get paid varies by job *and* by client, so I have to be diligent with my budget to ensure that I have enough money to pay the bills when they are due and hopefully have a little extra to spare.

In addition, I don't enjoy self-marketing. For example, each time I release a new book, I almost cringe when sharing it on social media. I don't want to be the person that everyone sees and turns the other way because they don't want to be sold something.

3. Would you advise a friend to become a freelancer or would you advise they get a normal 9 to 5 job? And why?

I would advise them to do whatever makes them most happy. As long as you have a job that you enjoy, you'll make the best of it and each option comes with its advantages and disadvantages.

That being said, if the person wasn't particularly self-motivated, I would probably recommend that they stick with a 9 to 5 because being self-employed requires being willing to push yourself…even when you don't want to.

4. What do you think is the best freelancing site and why?

I've only worked within a couple sites, but the freelance site that I currently get a majority of my jobs through is Elance. I've been with them long enough to have a high rank and over a third of my clients are repeat, making me proud of both of these accomplishments.

To me, Elance is easy to use and I love that I can set up to receive daily emails with jobs that fit parameters that I've created. They also offer escrow so that you can be sure that the money is there prior to starting a job, which adds a little bit of security.

Whether they are the best, I can't say. I think it depends on your own personal preferences and each site gets easier to use when you become more familiar with it and learn the ins and outs.

5. Have you ever picked up work outside of the freelance sites and if so how did you find this work?

Yes, I've picked up several wonderful freelance jobs outside of Elance, most of which I've found via various emails that I subscribe to (like Freelance Writing Jobs and Indeed) that list current freelance job postings. I also check out Craigslist from time to time just to see what is out there.

The one caveat is to be careful with jobs outside of freelance sites to make sure you get paid. Set up a payment schedule that allows you to receive payments in intervals so you don't find yourself completing a project and sweating about whether or not you'll ever see all of the money that you are owed.

6. Do you have any tips on how to win freelance jobs? (either on the freelance sites or outside of these).

The one thing that I think gets me some really good jobs is that I don't talk about myself a lot; instead, I tell my potential client what I can do for them. Sure, I share a little bit about my qualifications, but my number one goal with my proposals is to make them envision all of the wonderful things that will happen to them (like turning their prospective clients into paying customers) if they hire me.

7. Do you have any tips on how to accumulate good feedback on the freelance sites?

I think that one of the best ways to get good feedback is to under-promise and over-deliver. When clients are given more than what they expect to receive, they're very willing to share that information. For example, I generally give myself an extra day or two to complete a project so when the client gets it earlier than what they've anticipated, they are pleasantly surprised and ready to tell the world about it.

Plus, I leave *them* good feedback which helps entice them to do the same for me.

8. How do you keep your clients happy?

Other than under-promising and over-delivering, I also make whatever revisions to their work they want without getting offended and giving them attitude. I don't take their suggestions personally as

I understand that we all have different styles and mine may not be for them.

Additionally, I always keep a level of respect and professionalism with my clients. I treat them as if they are the only person I work for because a happy client will not only use your services in the future, but they'll also refer you to their colleagues, which is extremely important when you work for yourself.

9. Do you have any tips on how to effectively manage your time?

Realistically, the hardest part of time management for me involves getting family and friends to realize that even though I work from home, I do actually work. I can't go here and there with them or be tied up on the phone all day or I won't get paid.

Other than that, my best advice is to come up with a time management system that suits your personality and style. Personally, I don't set rigid work hours as I find that it drains my energy. I do set a kitchen timer though and work in 90 minute intervals making sure I get up when it goes off and do something else for a few minutes. This keeps me from getting burnt out by never taking a break.

10. Do you prefer working by yourself or is freelancing a lonely life?

I do prefer working by myself, but freelancing can definitely get lonely from time to time. To counter this, I work part time for my aunt at her bakery which is a great opportunity to get out and be social. I also think it makes me a better writer because you draw from your life experiences when you write. If you have none, it can be pretty hard to come up with new content. Plus, it keeps me sane.

11. Do you have any other tips for people who want to be successful freelancers?

I would say that if you want to be successful as a freelancer, be prepared to work countless hours to hone your craft. No matter how good you write, you will always write better the more you do it.

Also, you can't have thin skin. Some people will love your work and others will hate it, but it is important to remember that their opinions are reflective of their own personal preferences, not of whether you are "good" or not.

I always remind myself of Jack Canfield, co-author of the *Chicken Soup for the Soul* series. He was turned down by well over 100 different publishers before one finally accepted him and look how far his perseverance has taken him!

Finally, while it is important to learn how others have become successful as a freelancer, it is perhaps even more imperative that you find what works best for *you*. It is your uniqueness and individuality that will get you noticed, so you have to be willing to make your own footprints and create your own path if you want to stand out.

Gizelle Bichard

natural@telkomsa.net

Alternative health and spirituality freelance writer and researcher extraordinaire.

(I am a freelance writer so although some of my answers could apply to freelancing in general, most are specifically applicable to freelance writing.)

1. What do you enjoy about being a freelancer?

Freedom! If I want to work until midnight and sleep until noon, I can do it. I can work anywhere, anytime. I also love the variety of work and the ability to choose writing that is meaningful and interesting to me. I tend to concentrate on the jobs that will challenge me at least a little and I have learnt an enormous amount about myself in the process. One of the best things about freelancing though is the wonderful clients I have worked with from all over the world. I have done work for people in Morocco, Saudi, Turkey, Australia, United Kingdom, United States of America, Canada, Sweden, and Denmark and even in my own backyard, South Africa, whilst living in a tiny town near the tip of Africa. It's almost like travelling but I don't have to leave home.

2. What don't you enjoy about being a freelancer?

Yeah, well obviously it's not all wine and roses! Freelancing can be an uncertain and unpredictable game with the feast or famine scenario on a regular basis. I have had stretches of no work and then stretches where I was juggling way too many jobs at the same time. If one job is delayed or takes longer than expected or the client requests additional work that you can't refuse, things can start to pile up and get messy.

The other thing that I used to hate was the constant bidding on jobs. I have done hundreds of them, each one unique, with the full realization that I might be awarded a tiny percentage. However, once I had gathered enough positive feedback and had established myself, this aspect definitely got easier.

3. Would you advise a friend to become a freelancer or would you advise they get a normal 9 to 5 job? And why?

I have never had a normal 9 to 5 job so freelancing is a good fit for me. If someone needs security, predictability and accountability from an outside source, freelancing is probably not a good idea. My suggestion to anyone who thinks they would like to become a freelancer is to get their feet wet while they still have a job. It's a great life but there are very few people who become an overnight success.

4. What do you think is the best freelancing site and why?

I have worked on Elance for some time now and find that it suits me very well. I have tried other sites like People Per Hour, Constant Content, oDesk and a few others but either found the layouts confusing or the bid process unsatisfactory and never had much success with any of them. I am not saying they are bad sites, just not my cup of tea. I have friends who are quite happy with a couple of those sites but not with Elance.

Elance is a huge site and can be daunting at first but once you know your way around, it is awesome. I think it is extremely well run, professional and has good quality clients and contractors. They are well established and have good resources, training and information. There are tons of dreadful jobs on every site and Elance is no exception. These are the ones that pay stones but expect you to have a PhD and 25 hours a day to dedicate to their work which you will deliver in perfectly formatted and error free condition. I vet every client before I bid and pay attention to the feedback from previous contractors. Other than that, I trust my gut.

5. Have you ever picked up work outside of the freelance sites and if so how did you find this work?

Yes, I have had work referred to me by friends and I have answered local ads. I keep my eyes and ears open, talk to people who might need a writer and I have even sent emails to a couple of internet sites offering to rewrite their horribly worded and error ridden pages.

6. Do you have any tips on how to win freelance jobs? (either on the freelance sites or outside of these).

Bid, bid, bid! Answer adverts and get yourself out there. Be proactive and don't sit around waiting for jobs to fall into your lap. You have to be in it to win it. If you are just starting out, bid on anything and everything you think you can do, even if the budget is below what you think you are worth. Do a slap up job, get some great feedback and only then can you afford to be more picky.

When you bid, don't write your life story and don't waffle on about how good the job would be for you. Rather tell the client what you can do for them – big difference. Keep the proposals short and to the point whilst still addressing each and every point.

READ the job outline properly and tailor the bid accordingly. Yes, this takes time, lots of time, and it doesn't guarantee you will be awarded the job. However, if you can't perform this simple task, you are wasting everybody's time and you definitely won't get the job.

If you are going to send samples of your work, make sure they are relevant to the job at hand. If you are new and don't have any samples, write them specifically for the job.

Make sure your profile is error free – it's your store front and you don't want the very first sentence a prospective client sees, to put them off. Get somebody else to proof it for you.

These are the major bugbears that client's hate, gleaned from reading thousands of job posts.

- Canned proposals – these are pretty much like spam – don't use them

- Not bothering to read the instructions. For instance, the client requests samples but contractors don't attach them.

- Sloppy proposals with grammatical errors

7. Do you have any tips on how to accumulate good feedback on the freelance sites?

Always go the extra mile and over deliver where you can. If you can offer something that you see will add value to the finished product but is outside of the scope of your work, do it, especially if it won't take much time. Don't expect extra compensation for this though – it's about building good relationships.

Keep going back to the original job description to make sure you are on track. Remember "When all else fails, read the instructions."

Never be afraid to ask questions and to say you don't understand when something isn't crystal clear. Of course, if you accepted a job and agreed to certain requirements which you don't actually meet, there's always Google.

8. How do you keep your clients happy?

I do my best to be friendly, yet professional. I let the client take the lead but I ask for clarification often and am always open to revising work until the client is happy. I take real ownership of my writing but also recognise that it does not ultimately belong to me, so if a client disagrees with the tone or content, I change it without complaint. Freelancers can't be prima donnas.

Prompt communication is vital, especially if you live in a different time zone to your client. I am not suggesting you stay up all night but just that you answer emails as soon as you can and keep the client updated about your progress, even if there isn't any.

9. Do you have any tips on how to effectively manage your time?

Gosh, to be honest, no! I suppose treating freelancing like you would a 9 to 5 job, with the same hours and schedule, could work for some people but for me that would defeat the main purpose of freelancing in the first place. There are times when my brain just shuts down and I can't write a coherent sentence so I need to take advantage of the times when inspiration and creativity are back in town, and write – even if it's 3 am.

10. Do you prefer working by yourself or is freelancing a lonely life?

I like working on my own but it can get a bit lonely too. My worst jobs have been those where the response from the client has been minimal to non-existent and I felt like I was marooned all alone on a desert island. I perform much better with clients who keep in contact and find that it makes for a better product in the long run. Requests for editing, changes and rewording are far better than a total lack of communication.

I also find it helps to have relationships with other people who are in a similar line of work – that can make all the difference. I often send links to jobs that I think might suit friends and acquaintances and try to keep in touch with other freelancers.

11. Do you have any other tips for people who want to be successful freelancers?

If you really want to make it in the world of freelancing, be persistent, pay attention to detail and hone your skills. Above all, treat the client exactly the way you would want to be treated.

Sarah Laing

tikadiva1@hotmail.com

1. What do you enjoy about being a freelancer?

For me, being a freelancer is living out my childhood dream. I showed interest in writing at a very early age. Throughout my school years I wrote non-stop – about anything and everything. When I was at university, I began exploring the world of writing in a deeper way. I wanted to be a published author and I read every book I could, to learn about that process. But, life got in the way. I never stopped thinking about writing and in my late 20s it finally consumed me. I realized I couldn't live without writing. I decided to go for it. That's when I dove into the world of freelance writing and never looked back.

Aside from living out my childhood dream of writing for a living, I enjoy the challenge of freelance writing; it's not easy to write for a living, but it's so rewarding. You get to crawl into the minds of your clients, interpret their vision and make it come alive. There is no greater feeling than the pride you have when you see your finished work.

2. What don't you enjoy about being a freelancer?

Freelancing is not all lollipops and puppies. It's demanding and exhausting (especially when you're a Type A personality/perfectionist like myself). The time commitment is intense, but it's really all worth it. To succeed at anything, you have to put the work in.

There are two things that I have a hard time with. The first is receiving criticism. When you put your heart into a piece of work, you develop a sort of loyalty to it. When you receive criticism, you are forced to abandon, to a certain extent, something that you had, seemingly, perfected. What I've realized is that not everyone shares your vision or sees your direction. The second thing I have a hard time with, is not getting credit for my work. When I ghostwrite, I can't claim that as a credential. Although it would be nice to be acknowledged for all of my work, I continue to remind myself that experience is more valuable than a byline. We do it for the love of writing, right?

3. Would you advise a friend to become a freelancer or would you advise they get a normal 9 to 5 job? And why?

I absolutely would advise a friend to be a freelancer…if it were the right friend. I mean, you must have certain qualities to be a freelancer. You must be creative, hard-working, patient, driven…the list goes on. If that friend was looking to make fast money, freelancing is not the right path for them. If they were committed to building their brand and their experience, I would tell them to go for it.

I started freelancing while holding down a demanding full time job. It makes for long days, restricted weekends, and constant engagement, but I do it because it's worth it and because nothing makes me happier than writing. You have to want it for all the right reasons.

4. What do you think is the best freelancing site and why?

Elance! But, I'm 100% biased. Elance is the first and only freelancing site I have used. I fell in love with Elance the moment I landed my first job. Elance, for me, has been a great platform for not only writing, but for learning. I have learned so much about the freelance world and about myself. I love that I am able to create a virtual resume on Elance for everyone to see. In addition, the people at Elance are quick to answer questions and quick to resolve issues.

5. Have you ever picked up work outside of the freelance sites and if so how did you find this work?

I have. Before starting on Elance, I worked for an online magazine writing entertainment articles. Outside freelance work is available and you just have to find it. I googled things such as "call for writing submissions" and looked to the contributor sections of online magazines, which lead me to the job I eventually landed.

6. Do you have any tips on how to win freelance jobs? (either on the freelance sites or outside of these).

You have to treat every potential freelance job like an interview and an opportunity to sell yourself. You have to convince a potential client that you are what they are looking for and that your contribution will benefit them in some way. In order to do that there are several things you must present to the client. You must provide your credentials, your work experience and work samples that apply to the specific job. Try giving them a taste of what you can offer by telling them how you intend to approach the project or what topics you intend to cover. Try to connect with the client on a personal level. Do you have personal experiences that apply to the job? Can you identify with the client in a particular way? You will get the job if you set yourself apart from the pack.

7. Do you have any tips on how to accumulate good feedback on the freelance sites?

Good feedback is given to those who deserve it. There are, however, ways you can increase the likelihood of receiving favourable feedback.

Here are a few of those ways:

- NEVER WORK FOR A CLIENT WHO CONSISTENTLY GIVES POOR FEEDBACK. Such a client will give you poor feedback no matter what kind of quality you deliver. Accept that there are people who can't be pleased and move on.

- BE ÜBER RESPONSIVE. I have committed to responding to clients within the hour (not including while I'm sleeping). No one likes to wait and I can totally appreciate that.

- PUT IN THE EXTRA EFFORT. Go the extra mile to super-please the client. For example, send them updates on your progress when they aren't expecting it. I've also heard of freelancers who give nightly updates. Your effort will not go unnoticed and, more importantly, you will be remembered for future projects.

8. How do you keep your clients happy?

Apart from the point in Question #7, keeping your clients happy is really the easiest part of freelancing. There are 5 things you need to do to ensure everyone is happy.

- Listen to your clients and really hear them!

- Respond to your clients in a timely manner.

- Commit to working on a project until the client is satisfied.

- Don't ever, under any circumstances, deliver a late product. Fevered babies, emergency animal surgeries, failed internet connections … there are no excuses. Prepare for the worst.

- Go above and beyond in any way possible.

9. Do you have any tips on how to effectively manage your time?

I've become a master of time management, but that mastery did not come easily. I need to be in the zone if I am going to write to my full potential. I have learned that I need to turn off my phone, turn off the TV, turn off my iPad and turn off my husband. Distractions will cost you time and creativity. If you allot yourself a scheduled amount of uninterrupted time, you will get things done.

10. Do you prefer working by yourself or is freelancing a lonely life?

I am lucky in that my day job gives me the human contact and the break from writer's block that every freelance writer can benefit from. I would, however, embrace a full-time freelancing lifestyle. In order to avoid the crazy, I think it's important to have tools in place to connect with the outside world. For example, instead of emailing my clients, I often Skype with them. It allows for a personal connection and it also allows for quick, clear and concise communication.

11. Do you have any other tips for people who want to be successful freelancers?

Writers make up a unique group of individuals. If you are not a writer, it's difficult to understand someone who wants to and needs to write for a living. If you want to become a freelancer, you have to learn to ignore the people in your life who don't identify with your dreams and your goals. I am lucky enough to have people in my life that support me and want me to follow my dreams. I also have people in my life who don't get it. I have chosen to prove those people wrong by setting goals and committing to achieving those goals. And, even if I don't achieve those goals, I'm doing what I love and what I was meant to do. Life is too short to forgo the things you love.

Once you get into the freelance world, you have to immediately start building relationships and networking. This can be done in many ways and here are a couple:

- USE SOCIAL MEDIA. Social media is under-utilized by a lot of freelancers. Sign up for Twitter, Facebook, Pinterest, Instagram, etc. Let people know you are a fixture in the business.

- DON'T JUST STICK TO THE FREELANCE SITES. Add some spice to your life and mix things up. Try entering writing competitions. Competitions give you a chance to write and to hone your craft. Recently I entered a poetry writing competition. I had never written poetry and never had the urge to. But, the prompt that was given inspired me to write. I didn't win the competition, or even place in the top 10, but I gave it a shot and had a great time doing it.

Freelancing is an ever-evolving world, and I think the only thing that can make life easier for a freelancer is to keep up with that evolution. If you are dedicated and ahead of the game, your life as a freelancer will get easier with time. Here are a few key ways to keep up in the crazy, fast-paced world of freelance:

- COMMIT TO CONTINUED EDUCATION. Try taking courses and attending workshops. I am a freelance writer with extensive experience in article and creative writing, editing, proofreading, formatting, rewriting and ghost-writing. I just got into writing e-books and am learning about the ins and outs of those. I have also committed to learning about copywriting, which has always been of interest to me. Being a one-trick pony in the freelance world will get you nowhere fast. Expanding your knowledge will make your freelance experience a smoother and more rewarding one.

∞ LOOK TO YOUR SURROUNDINGS FOR INSPIRATION. Pay attention to your surroundings. We, as freelancers, have a tendency to work on autopilot, counting on our creative minds to come up with an endless flow of never-before-seen-or-heard ideas. Eventually, your creativity will dull and so will your writing. Look to your surroundings for inspiration. I always have my notepad open on my iPhone for that flash of genius that hits me at the most unexpected times.

∞ TAKE ADVANTAGE OF YOUR DOWNTIME. Treat your downtime as bonus time. Just because you don't have work, doesn't mean you don't have to work. When I have slow days (a.k.a. bonus days), I spend them doing the following:

A) CATCHING UP ON SOCIAL MEDIA. I tweet, read pertinent information (and not tabloid garbage) and make connections. I also make sure that I follow all my clients on Twitter so I can show an interest in their brand and get a sense of who they are.

B) TOUCHING BASE WITH PAST CLIENTS. I like to let them know I am available for work and that I enjoyed working with them in the past.

C) WORKING ON ELANCE. I apply for as many jobs as I can, I update my profile, I take skills tests and I organize my workroom.

D) WRITING. Just because you don't have to write, doesn't mean you shouldn't. Write about whatever comes to your mind. Submit your work to online magazines and other freelancing opportunities.

A freelancer's work is never done!

Daniel Hall

www.blogtrepreneur.co.uk

1. What do you enjoy about being a freelancer?

There are a number of things I enjoy about being a freelancer but none more so than being able to choose which clients I work for. Before I pitch for a job I look at what the potential client has written in their listing to work out what kind of person they are. If they say something along the lines of "I want immediate success...", then I don't bid on the job because that particular client has unrealistic expectations. Secondly, I always talk to the client before accepting to take on their work so I can judge their character. Finally, if I take on a client and they do end up to be a pain in the back side, then I drop them as a client. This allows me to have a stress free life compared to my previous job where we had a few awful clients that would make life hell for anyone that had to deal with them.

Freelancing allows me freedom with my hours. I can work when I want and this allows me to walk the dogs, find time for the gym and have the occasional day off when the sun comes out!

Money wise freelancing is perfect too. For my age and experience I was pretty well paid at my old job but this year I'm on course to triple what I was earning. This only happens because I work hard and I'm good at what I do but it allows me to not have to worry about money anymore.

Being able to work from home (or from anywhere in the world for that matter) is great. I don't have to spend money on transport, I don't have to spend ages getting ready every day and if I wanted to move abroad I could do so without it impacting my work at all.

2. What don't you enjoy about being a freelancer?

Like anything in life there are disadvantages to being a freelancer. The biggest downside is that if you don't work you don't get paid. So if you are unwell, then you either take time off and don't earn any money, or you work through the illness. For those who are employed at a company, they can take time off when they are ill and still be paid. Similarly it's very hard for me to take a holiday because I receive emails from clients every day asking me to do things and I do daily management of my clients' Adwords accounts. If I were to go on a holiday then I could easily end up losing a lot of clients. Again, if I were to work for a company then I could take paid holiday without having to worry.

Secondly it's a very lonely job. In an office you are surrounded by people and can have general chit chat. When you work from home by yourself you have no interaction with anyone; exception for email exchanges with clients about work. Sometimes this lack of interaction can make you depressed.

It's also, a very 'hit and miss' thing. The majority of the time I am being offered six or seven jobs per day but I still come across the odd week every now and again when the market is dead and I may only pick up one job for the week.

Finally freelancing can take over your life. It makes you money hungry so you end up working every hour under the sun and you feel bad if you are not working. It becomes an unhealthy obsession. When you work for a company, normally when you finish work your day is over and you can relax. Relaxing is a rarity for a freelancer.

3. Would you advise a friend to become a freelancer or would you advise they get a normal 9 to 5 job? And why?

I would definitely recommend it to my friends and as a result of doing just that, a few of my friends are now freelancers. Most people want to be in control of their destiny and what they earn. Freelancing gives you those privileges.

But, as I have told my friends who have started freelancing, it's extremely hard to get a foot in the door. Until you accumulate a lot of good feedback it's hard to be picky over which clients you work for. It's also much harder to pick up work and therefore financially it can be a struggle at the beginning. This should only be the case for a few months but when things are not going your way immediately, it's very easy to just say it isn't working and go back to getting a normal job. To make freelancing a career, you therefore need resilience and patience. Once you have got over this initial hurdle, life becomes much, much easier and you begin to see the benefits of being a freelancer.

As they say, patience is a virtue and I regularly see new freelancers bidding on tons of jobs for a week or two. After that you never see them again. I would assume they get disheartened by bidding for so many jobs and not being awarded any, and therefore think freelancing isn't for them. Let me assure you, once you get one job it becomes much easier to pick up that second job, and so on.

It may be a good idea to start freelancing as a side line whilst you are employed. This would allow you to accumulate enough feedback to be able to confidently quit your job and begin working as a freelancer without having to go through the initial period of pain.

4. What do you think is the best freelancing site and why?

Definitely Elance. Out of all the freelance sites it has the most new jobs posted and the quality of the jobs is much higher than those posted on other freelance sites. It's also very easy to use and if you do have any issues the customer service team usually resolve them for you very quickly.

I used to use People Per Hour when I first started freelancing but unfortunately, there are just not enough jobs posted on the site to make it worth my time browsing it. As a result it takes a very long time to build up feedback on the site – which is what helps you win jobs. If you are just starting out then it may be worth using People Per Hour as it increases the overall number of jobs that you can bid on. The lack of jobs is the only thing that lets People Per Hour down as a site.

oDesk and Freelancer.com from my experience seem to have the lowest quality of jobs posted. These are the sites where clients expect you to work for $2 per hour. This may be OK if you are living in a third world country but it's just not feasible for anyone who lives in the West.

5. Have you ever picked up work outside of the freelance sites and if so how did you find this work?

I freelance in Pay Per Click advertising and I won my first job by doing tons of searches on Google. I typed in practically anything and saw what adverts came up. If I spotted any badly written adverts or adverts containing spelling mistakes, then I contacted the company in question. I explained why I had contacted them specifically, and asked if they wanted a free review of their account. I picked up work through this method but it's a very time consuming way of going about things and as a result I just stick to the freelance sites now.

Word of mouth is the other big way. I've picked up a number of clients on the freelance sites who have told their friends / business contacts about me. They ultimately email me and I end up doing work for them.

I have also had a number of people who have found me via my LinkedIn profile. Because on my profile I highlight my results and feedback that I have received from people, I pick up jobs on there. So make sure your LinkedIn profile is up to date.

6. Do you have any tips on how to win freelance jobs? (either on the freelance sites or outside of these).

Always make your proposals personal. Explain why you would be a good fit for the job by actually mentioning parts from the job description. This shows you have read it and understand what needs to be done. Unfortunately there are tons of people out there who apply for all jobs using a standard proposal and in the majority of cases clients see straight through this and don't hire you as a result.

If you have good feedback, then highlight this fact and ask the client in your proposal to review your feedback. This gives the reader more confidence in you.

Try to stand out from the crowd – when I first started off I would offer free reviews of the clients Adwords account and this used to win me a lot of work. I've passed the stage of needing to do this now but when I was starting off it gave me an edge on the competition. Remember – people love something that is free. I can also give another good example of this. When posting a job up for a website I wanted to have created, one freelancer sent me a logo he had designed for the site. He didn't charge me for this but used it as an example of what he could do. I went on to choose the freelancer because of that and have used him several times since. If you go the extra mile then you should win work.

Finally think about starting a blog. I wrote a number of blog posts when I worked for my company a few years ago. They are outdated now and were not even written for this purpose, but I always put links to them in my proposal and lots of people choose me because of them. The advice I give in the blog posts portrays me as an expert and that is the kind of freelancer that people are looking to work with.

7. Do you have any tips on how to accumulate good feedback on the freelance sites?

Similarly to when you bid for the job, go the extra mile when actually working on it. Clients appreciate effort.

When I complete a job I always write a 2 or 3 page document which outlines what I have done and why. It adds an extra unpaid hour to each job but this document allows me to answer any questions a client may have before they ask it, and tells the client what a wonderful job I have done for them. Not every client reads the document but the ones that do are always very happy.

I also follow a trick that retail sites use. When someone purchases a product some retail sites ask the customer to leave a review about their site on the different review sites around the web. Obviously the customer has yet to receive the product but the website marketers assume that the customer was happy with their experience when using the site. As a result, the customer leaves feedback when they were happy with their experience and this culminates in good reviews. If the website owners were to wait a few weeks before asking for feedback then it gives the customer an opportunity to become unhappy. The product might have got damaged in the post, arrived late or was different than described. Asking for feedback before any of this can happen means the websites accumulate much better feedback. I use this approach for my freelancing feedback. As soon as I have built campaigns for clients I ask them to leave feedback. At this stage they do not know how they will perform but having read the document that I've prepared which explains the work produced, they are usually happy to leave me a good review. Unfortunately about 30% of clients want to wait a few weeks before leaving feedback – but if you have done a good job then in the long term you have nothing to worry about as you should still get good feedback then.

I am also very selective about my clients. I always look at the feedback that potential clients have left for others in the past. There are lots of potential clients out there, whose feedback history shows they have never left any positive feedback. Some people cannot be pleased and it's likely no matter how good a job you do, you will also receive poor feedback from them. Feedback is your display shop window, so don't be afraid to turn down these clients. Doing so earns you a lot more money in the long run. If you take these clients on you will get bad feedback and this is incredibly hard (sometimes even impossible) to recover from. I usually turn down offers of work from about 15 potential clients per week due to this.

Finally, be selective not only with clients but the jobs themselves. I regularly get invited to bid or am asked to take on jobs that have no chance of success. There are tons of people out there who will take these jobs on but I always decline. If a job is destined to failure then why allow yourself to get bad feedback because of it? I'm always courteous and explain to the client that what they want will not work because of X, Y and Z. Sometimes these people listen and save themselves a fortune, other times they don't listen and end up wasting tons of money. Essentially, it's not your problem what these people decide to do after you decline the job but just make sure you are not the one that takes it on.

8. How do you keep your clients happy?

This is a recurring theme here, but I always go the extra mile. Even if it causes me more work I will suggest changes that can be made to campaigns to improve them. I try to offer advice in other areas as well. So I might explain that if they improved a certain aspect of their website it would mean that their Pay Per Click would improve.

Try to make friends with your clients. When you have a personal relationship with a client it makes things much easier.

I also always reply to messages quickly which shows that I'm on top of anything that needs to be done.

9. Do you have any tips on how to effectively manage your time?

Don't take on clients that seem to dither. If clients ask me more than 4 questions after I pitch for a job then I decline the chance to work with them. If a client asks to Skype or call you to discuss the project then decline the opportunity to work with them. This may seem silly from the outside but I say this with experience. Every single client that I have taken on, who asks numerous questions before a campaign begins or wishes to discuss the project, has turned out to be time wasters. By this I mean these clients will continue to ask two or three questions every week. When you become a busy freelancer you realise that your biggest commodity is time. If you take on client who wastes a few hours of your time each week, then you are losing time that you could better spend elsewhere working on projects. If you are answering emails you are not earning money. The clients who just award you the job without asking questions very rarely cause you any issues and as a result you are much more productive by taking such clients on.

10. Do you prefer working by yourself or is freelancing a lonely life?

As mentioned previously, one of the disadvantages of freelancing is that it can be an incredibly lonely career path. Some people prefer working by themselves but I'm sure after a while even these people wish they had someone to talk to during the day.

11. Do you have any other tips for people who want to be successful freelancers?

Watch out for burnout. I've yet to meet a freelancer who hasn't experienced burnout. When you first start out you want to work every hour under the sun. In my first few months I was working over

100 hours per week and this took a real toll. My memory started to go (which is one of my strongest assets) and it was only after a few months that I realised it was burnout that I was experiencing. I took a step back for a week and after that I was fine again. If your body is telling you that you are overworking yourself then you probably are – and in the long term this is not good for you. You know your body better than anyone else, so try not to over extend yourself too much. This will lead to you producing better work, working faster and making fewer mistakes.

Stay on top of your invoices. At the start of each month I print off my invoices from the previous month. This means that at the end of the tax year I do not have to spend a few days printing off different invoices. Doing it this way should mean you don't forget any invoices / expenses either.

Always work through the freelance sites. It may cost you a percentage of what you earn but it's very easy to get stung if you work outside of the freelance sites. One of my first clients wanted to work outside of one of the sites. I agreed and did a lot of work for him. He didn't pay me and it took a good 6 months and the start of legal proceedings to get the money I was owed. It's stress that you don't need and takes valuable time away from you if this happens. Don't risk it. Do all your work through freelance sites and feel secure that you will get paid.

Put in as much effort as possible for potential clients who say they are an agency. If you pick these up as clients and do a good job, it's likely that you will get tons of other projects from them in the future.

Sarah Ratliff

http://coquiprose.com/

1. What do you enjoy about being a freelancer?

The list is long. After more than 25 years in corporate America, although I am grateful because I learned a lot and I gained valuable experience, it was time to start my own business. Although not an exhaustive list, to follow are several of the things I love about freelancing:

- I love setting my own hours

- I love the ability to grow my business on my own terms

- I love being able to establish and maintain relationships with my clients, again, on my own terms (not those of the corporation who employs me)

- I love being able to wear (or shoot, not wear) whatever I please to work

- When I am restless, have writer's block or just need a change of scenery, I can go play with my goats or dogs (my husband and I own an organic farm)

- I have a treadmill instead of a desk, and I love being able to walk while I work

- I have my iPod next to my computer, and I listen to whatever I want, when I want to listen to it. I don't have to be concerned with bothering my coworkers with music that doesn't fit in with their taste. I can listen to it as loudly or softly as I like as well. And the best part is that if I want to sing along with the music, I don't have to hear about the comparisons between my voice and the worst torture anyone's ever had to endure. ☺

∞ I love being able to mentor new freelancers who come to me with questions about how they too can do what I do/have done.

2. What don't you enjoy about being a freelancer?

Any of the aspects I don't enjoy about freelancing are ones I have control over and that I can change. For example, if I have a client who isn't good about respecting my boundaries (calling at inappropriate hours or on holidays), I can "fire" that client. If I am struggling to find work/life balance, I am in control of that. I honestly can't list anything I don't like or a downside to freelancing. I suppose I wished I'd started doing it years earlier.

3. Would you advise a friend to become a freelancer or would you advise they get a normal 9 to 5 job? And why?

Yes and no. Having now been a freelancer for the last 5 years, I have seen many freelancers come and go. This isn't exactly an easy job. It involves skills that many don't have and they haven't considered needing, and if they haven't acquired them by this point, it might be difficult to find success. Among the skills I speak of are marketing, sales, customer service and project management (ability to manage several projects simultaneously and not drop the ball on any of them). It also requires patience, maturity, a thick skin, ability to learn from mistakes (there will be a lot growing pains and scraped knees) and lastly it helps to have an outgoing personality.

It also takes "sticktoitiveness," drive and a bit of "I absolutely can't fail no matter how tough things get!" It also takes luck, the ability to not personalize things, as well as knowing when to fall on one's sword, and lastly, an ability to read people. Not everyone has any of these skills, and so it's not for everyone. I have advised some of my friends to consider freelancing and found myself regretting it because they lacked one, a few or all of the skills I think are necessary to be successful in this business. If only it were a matter of having talent in a particular area.

4. What do you think is the best freelancing site and why?

Of course it's Elance. I was signed up with Scriptlance (believe it's now owned by another company) and they sucked. Yes, I am blunt. I registered with Freelancer, oDesk and Guru and frankly they made me long for Scriptlance. I haven't done anything with my profile on any of them. Elance has the best combination of clients willing to pay fairly decent rates (this has started to change in last year) and desire to continue improving infrastructure.

5. Have you ever picked up work outside of the freelance sites and if so how did you find this work?

Outside of Scriptlance, no.

6. Do you have any tips on how to win freelance jobs? (either on the freelance sites or outside of these).

Stop, read, digest and understand the job description. Address clients' concerns in a proposal and don't tell clients what you think they want to hear. After addressing clients' concerns, explain step-by-step or even high level how this can be achieved. Come across with the right balance of confidence and humility – cockiness and lack of confidence in oneself and one's abilities are huge turn offs. Be clear in all communications (both oral and written) and say what you do, and do what you say.

7. Do you have any tips on how to accumulate good feedback on the freelance sites?

That's simple:

- Deliver great work
- Under promise and over deliver
- Partner with clients (we aren't employees and clients aren't employers; we are equals)
- Don't think of this as a chop shop where you're always thinking about the next job while in the middle of the present one. Focus on what's in front of you and deliver the best you can. Think of ways you can continue working together in the future. I'd rather have five clients for whom all on my team work, than 50 clients who never want to work with us again and we have to continually find new work.
- Be proud of the work you deliver – always - or don't deliver it.
- If a client forgets or doesn't think it's important to leave feedback, ask – professionally and politely.

8. How do you keep your clients happy?

I could write a long list of ways I make my clients happy but it comes down to one thing – I partner with my clients. Their success is my success and vice versa.

If you mess up (and it happens), be willing to fall on your sword.

9. Do you have any tips on how to effectively manage your time?

Learn your limitations and don't push yourself beyond them. Don't "bite off more than you can chew." I don't think anyone really can manage time. I learned in the corporate world that it's a fallacy. We strive to, but we can't. We do the best we can and when we fall short, we don't beat ourselves up and try to improve. When I say we, I mean successful people.

10. Do you prefer working by yourself or is freelancing a lonely life?

By nature I am extremely gregarious and outgoing. I am not really suited for being a writer. How I am able to serve both masters (be the introvert needed to be a writer and serve my need to be an extrovert) is to own a business where I communicate with my teammates and my clients. I don't allow my job to consume me. I also own a farm (as I mentioned) and stop to play with goats and/or dogs. I leave the farm every few days to get that social time in I crave.

11. Do you have any other tips for people who want to be successful freelancers?

Be realistic. I saw success very quickly and that's not the norm. Understand it won't happen overnight. I have a bit of a type A personality and because of personal reasons, we (my husband and I) couldn't afford for me to fail at freelancing. We didn't have that luxury. I look back several years ago and think I had a lot of chutzpah doing what I did. I feel like I am always ahead of the curve in terms of freelancing. I keep being able to take things to the next level and I think these are all important if freelancers want to see success. On Elance, or elsewhere, there are hundreds of thousands of freelancers all vying for the same jobs. Why blend and go for the same job? As soon as you can, find your niche, market yourself in that niche (or niches), and be the best, the most sought after and just go for it. I love Apple's motto, "Be Different," because it describes me to a T. I don't try and compete with the masses. I stand out in a crowd and distinguish myself. I take chances and I am different. I always strive to improve not only in the way I do business but in how I partner with my clients. I give them what they need before they even know they need it. I make myself invaluable to them. That's how you'll make it in this business – not by vying for the same sorry jobs. And continue to raise your rates. Don't be fearful of doing that.

I don't allow myself to be bound by limitations. I could tell you that because I don't have a college education, I shouldn't be as successful as I am. That's hogwash. I could tell you that I don't have enough money. That's also hogwash. I could tell you there aren't enough hours in the day, another tale of woe. In this business, we are only bound by personal limitations. There's a computer screen between us and our clients. If you don't feel you're pretty enough or smart enough or have the proper equipment, those are self-fulfilling prophecies and you'll never get anywhere. Figure out what you have control over and work to jump over those hurdles. If there are structural things (say with Elance) that are presenting challenges for you, find the appropriate person at Elance and address it with him or her. Nobody is going to hold your hand through this. You may find a mentor who can help you when you're at a fork in the road and aren't sure which way to go, but he/she isn't going to tell you how to go through steps A and B. If you want it, go for it. If you're not seeing the jobs you want on Elance, sit down and think through clearly what types of jobs you need to make the living you need and either approach Elance with your suggestion or do your research to find the clients you need.

Competition is fierce, but that's only an excuse not to make it.

Joost Doevelaar

http://www.linkedin.com/profile/view?id=77174063

1. What do you enjoy about being a freelancer?

The greatest thing about being a freelancer is the sense of freedom. If I do not feel like working right that minute, I can reschedule my work for later, unless I have a specific deadline that I have to meet. If I want to get to work at 6 AM or 9 PM, I am able to do so. I get to use the moments that I am most productive, that I feel inspired. This means that I produce better work.

Even though the money that I earn fluctuates, the money is usually pretty good. Especially if you are starting to become recognized as someone who delivers quality work every single time, it means that your value increases.

One final aspect about freelancing that I really enjoy is the fact that I can work on a number of different jobs. I find that I tend to get bored when I write about the same subject at length. I generally like to stick to a maximum of ten articles about the same topic – otherwise I find that I get bored and start to become less interested in the work itself. I know that if I am not fully invested in an article, it starts to wear on me and I have a hard time giving it my all. For one article I will be writing about fitness or healthy meals, and for the next article I may be writing about immigration reform. It gives me a chance to learn about new things that I would otherwise never have known about.

I also get a chance to talk to a number of different people; more often than not you end up with a solid relationship with your client. I have a repeat rate of over 30 percent, which to me means that I am doing something right. There is something rewarding about knowing that they have thousands of other freelancers at their disposal but they want to work with you again.

2. What don't you enjoy about being a freelancer?

I really enjoy the variety of topics that I get to write about, but I do not necessarily appreciate the variety of 'bosses' that you have. Some people have very specific rules about writing. They will expect you to emulate their writing style. Not just get close, but emulate it precisely. This can be especially challenging if you are working with someone for the first time.

Miscommunication can be another major issue. If I place my estimate for the job at three days, that means that between now and three days, to me, that means I am going to deliver the articles in your inbox. For some, that apparently means that they have to ask me about the articles several hours later. It can also be incredibly frustrating if you work with clients who say that they do not like something, but cannot tell you what is wrong with the work. I am all for making sure that the client is always happy, but if you give no feedback on what you would like me to change it becomes exceedingly difficult to fix something.

It is also frustrating to have people treat you as though they are your sole employer. When you are working with me and paying me, you are entitled to a great piece of writing that you are happy with. However, you are not entitled to all of my attention just because you are *one* of my clients. People should not expect me to drop everything else that I am doing just because they are willing to pay for an article. With some people, you are actually glad that you are just a freelancer and not their actual employee.

Finally, the money can be up and down. Sometimes you have to go below what you would normally charge just because you have not found a new client for a few days. Despite the fact that I have a network that provides me with steady work, I always want to find more clients I am able to work with. Some weeks will be great while other weeks I find that I am competing with some of the lower bids just to be able to get some income.

3. Would you advise a friend to become a freelancer or would you advise they get a normal 9 to 5 job?

To me, this choice depends on the person asking the question. Are you comfortable with having to find your own work? Do you believe in your own work to the point where it is the sole reason that people are going to come to you? You may be able to fool a few people the first week, but if you continuously produce mediocre work, chances are that you are going to be out of clients rather quickly. One of the main reasons that I am doing well is because of my constant flow of positive feedback. I make sure that people are happy with the work I produce, because that is what makes me stand out.

If you need a steady, guaranteed income, 9 to 5 is certainly better for most people. I have been doing this for years and my income is still not guaranteed. Yet the primary reason I started freelancing is because I was unable to get a 9 to 5, despite the fact that I had my Master's Degree in Communication. There are pros and cons to both sides.

4. What do you think is the best freelancing site and why?

I have yet to find a better site than Elance. Even though it takes a good chunk of my income, (approximately eight percent and then still demands a monthly fee) it does offer me the safety of escrow and allows me to build up a network where happy clients are able to leave me feedback. That is invaluable for both parties – my future clients see that I have been doing this for a long time and I am dedicated to my work, and I get to make sure that I am paid. Some of the other alternatives on the market do not have a great interface or just do not offer the same security. I am comfortable with offering eight percent of my income if it provides me with something extra, which is what I think I get from Elance.

5. Have you ever picked up work outside of the freelance sites?

I have, but most of the time it comes from people I already talked to on the freelance sites. It may be a referral of a client I talked to before or someone who reads a blog that I posted somewhere. That does not happen very often though. I am currently in the process of starting my own website, so it will hopefully increase the odds of this happening.

6. Do you have any tips on how to win freelance jobs?

Learn that sometimes you should not try to compete with others. If someone offers me a job and says they want 10 x 500 word articles for $20 I send them a pleasant email that thanks them for their interest, but that also lets them know that I am unable to accept. You have to remember that some people are going to want nothing more than words on paper. They may hire Indian or Pakistani writers for about 1/10th of what I would charge.

Make sure that you offer value for your product. You can go below what your estimated value is to start building up a network (if you are starting out) as long as you make it obvious that what you are offering is an introductory price. I found this out the hard way – if you are going to try to compete with some of the lowest bids and still try to deliver quality work, chances are that you will become frustrated fast.

7. Do you have any tips on how to accumulate good feedback on the freelance sites?

Communication remains vitally important when it comes to working with your clients. My clients come back to me because they know that if something is wrong for whatever reason, if something is not going according to their demands, I will revise it at no extra charge. That has limits of course, but I still make sure that every client

I have feels valued, big or small. I also make sure to leave feedback for them, lay out clear expectations they can hold me to and I never say anything ambiguous; I make everything clear.

As far as getting good feedback when you are just starting out? Do a few smaller jobs at first. Make sure that people get a chance to see your quality instead of having to rely on your word (because no one is going to admit that they produce mediocre work). If that means lowering your price to get an 'in'… so be it. Just as long as you know that your value has to increase afterwards.

8. How do you keep your clients happy?

I have touched on this a bit, but I make sure that my customer is always right. If there is something that I did not do right or if there is something that they want (whether they originally communicated it or not) I try to make sure that I make it right.

Another simple suggestion that I always follow is 'never to assume'. If I am unclear on something that my client said, I am not going to assume that he or she "meant this." I am going to ask them about it. If there is something that is misspelled or looks out of context, I ask them about it instead of assuming. Yes, it may mean that you get paid a day or two later because your client needs to read your email first, but there is nothing as negative as your client reading the delivered work and hating it or feeling as though you are not listening to their instructions. If you deliver shoddy work the first time around, you are always at a disadvantage. Even if your next revision is great, that original first impression that you made is negative. So if I am ever unsure about something, I ask.

Finally, I always make sure to adhere to my deadlines. I usually give myself a deadline of three days but deliver within 48 hours. In the event that I am unable to meet my deadline, I always make sure to communicate this with my client the second that it becomes obvious to me. There are few things more frustrating to clients than 'not knowing'. Yes, having to deliver your work late stinks, but it is 100 times better than the client not having the work and being left to wonder whether you are going to complete it or not.

9. Do you have any tips on how to effectively manage your time?

Make sure that you have a different mindset about work and play, especially if you work from home. Some people get dressed up before they work from home; I refuse to do that because I think it is silly. But I do make sure that I have a different view on work and play. I use the same computer for both, but I have to have a different mindset otherwise I am going to be distracted.

I also make sure that I have a little checklist of what needs to be done and when it needs to be done by. I just write this out on paper because there is something rewarding about crossing out a task with your pen. I make sure to prioritise my available tasks that way.

10. Do you prefer working by yourself or is freelancing a lonely life?

Honestly, it does feel good to be alone sometimes. I like not having people around me to distract me when I am doing research or am writing, especially those people who have questions every five minutes or who need to listen to music during the workday. That distracts me so I am unable to do as well on my tasks. However, if you do not make sure that you are social too, it is very easy to become a loner if you are a freelancer. Most people interact with their friends through school, sports, church, or work. If you cut out work altogether, you have to make an active effort to remain sociable.

11. Do you have any other tips for people who want to be successful freelancers?

If you are going to be a freelancer, just remember that people will often tell their friends about positive experiences, but they *ALWAYS* tell them about negative experiences. Whether you do this part-time or full-time, whatever you do, just make sure you put in your best work. I have never delivered something to a client where I felt that it was "good enough"… I always make sure to proofread my own work again after completing it. It is important that if it has my name on it, if I am being paid for it, it needs to be good. If you are just doing this to make a quick buck, just remember that people are able to tell the difference.

Brenda (B.K.) Walker

Freelance Writer and Editor
www.besthirefreelance.com

1. What do you enjoy about being a freelancer?

As a freelancer, I control my own financial destiny. It is my choice how much work to take on in any given period. I am not bound to the conventional time constraints often associated with the "Brick and Mortar/9-to-5" employment requirements. If I need to set an appointment in the middle of the day, then I do so. I have no supervisor to seek out for approval, nor a form that must be filled out in order to be paid for the time I am not at my desk. I merely adjust my time-table to reflect the gap I will be away for, notify my clients that I will be away for a period, turn on the answering devices, and go do what needs to be done.

I also truly love that I have the opportunity to pick-and-choose my projects. Freelancing allows me to expand my knowledgebase without others hovering over me. If I get it wrong the first time, I have the opportunity to fix my mistakes before anyone is even aware that I had to do some research in order to complete the task. Now my opportunities are endless.

2. What don't you enjoy about freelancing?

Right off the top of my head, it really infuriates me that some people do not recognize that what I do is a job. I have responsibilities and deadlines which must be met, just like anyone else who is working. Yes, I set my own schedule, but if I want to be paid, the job still has to be done. I cannot just "willy-nilly" run off and have a liquid lunch with friends, visit on the phone or Skype without setting aside the time.

The other "not-so-great" side of freelancing is that I don't have a guaranteed income. If I take a week off from work, there is no vacation pay waiting to compensate me. If I am sick, well, either I must work through the illness or sub-contract the work to another freelancer and lose the money. I don't believe in keeping a portion of the pay, as a "finder's fee," when I have to use a sub-contractor when I am unable to do the work myself. I bid for a job based upon the effort, knowledge, and skill it will require to complete the task with the best possible outcome and quality. That didn't change because I won't be the one doing the work.

3. Would you advise a friend to become a freelancer or would you advise they get a normal 9 to 5 job? And why?

Freelancing is definitely not for everyone. At this juncture and depending upon the economy, if you have a job, you should probably hang on to it, even if you aren't happy with the work situation. Remember that saying, "A bird in the hand...," well that most certainly applies. You wouldn't jump out of an airplane without a parachute, now would you?

Still, depending upon the circumstances, if a friend of mine was unable to, at the very least, find a good paying job, then I would and have suggested freelancing. There are a number of viable options in the world of freelancing that beat the heck out of going hungry. It is also a great way to keep your skills intact and maybe even learn one or two more in the process.

4. What do you think is the best freelancing site and why?

When I first began freelancing, there weren't any real platforms for freelance writers and editors. Instead, I sent query letters to viable sources, contacted marketing firms, and so on. In those days, freelancing was more of a platform for computer programmers and web designers.

Thank goodness, freelancers now have several options to choose from in finding viable work. I've tried several platforms/websites, but Elance is most certainly my favourite website to use. It is organized, inexpensive, and most importantly...trustworthy. The platform is extremely user friendly and they provide a real live person to talk to if you have a problem.

I believe that Elance takes all of the necessary steps to protect both the client and the freelancer. They also provide learning tools and how-to guides to help both parties understand how to be successful on the website. The same cannot be said for other platforms/websites.

5. Have you ever picked up work outside of the freelance sites and if so how did you find this work?

As I said before, there was a time when there really weren't any freelance sites that offered work for writers and editors. Even though there are several websites to choose from now, I still send out query letters to local media sources, as well as better-known newspapers, magazines, and other websites. Just because the world operates from more of a "digital" approach, don't rule out the "printed" resources.

I also have two websites, besthirefreelance.com, and one with the National Association of Independent Writers and Editors (NAIWE), brendawalker.naiwe.com. Both of these websites have brought me quite a bit of business outside of the freelancer platforms. They contain my profile, contact information, portfolio, and blog postings.

Of course, social media plays a big part in finding work. LinkedIn is a great resource for freelancers. I also post my work on my Facebook page as well as tweet links to my articles. Never underestimate the power of networking, handing out business cards, and referrals from friends, business associates, and clients.

6. Do you have any tips on how to win freelance jobs? (Either on the freelance sites or outside of these).

Wow, now that's a really good question with a rather long answer; but I'll try to be brief. It is important to compose your "bid" in a word document so that you can catch your errors and format appropriately. Consider this much as you would a cover letter for your résumé. Introduce yourself, explain why you are the perfect candidate for the job, and briefly describe any experience you have in that specific area.

You must, must, must have a professional portfolio that evidences your work. If you are new to freelancing and don't have "actual" examples, then get busy creating some. Your portfolio shows that you don't just talk the talk, but you walk the walk.

Don't get greedy, but in the same turn, don't under bid. Under bidding is a sign of desperation (even if you are desperate for work, try not to wear it like a neon sign). Clients want to know that you are confident in your work and you do that by bidding competitively and competently. It's a balancing act.

7. Do you have any tips on how to accumulate good feedback on the freelance sites?

Feedback is very important on the freelance sites. This is equivalent to references for conventional 9 to 5 jobs. When you finish a job, send the client a message that reminds them to fill out the feedback form and you will do the same for them. Freelancing is a two-way street. As important as it is for you to have good feedback, the same applies to clients. A client with poor feedback from freelancers is just as damaging as back feedback from a client. So make this a priority for you when you turn in your final work. You may have to remind the client more than once, that's okay, but if you have sent them three messages and they are still not responding, go ahead and fill out your side of the feedback…maybe even mention in your feedback a little something about how busy you know this client can be at times. This might prompt them to go ahead and fill out the feedback form for you.

8. How do you keep clients happy?

I live and work by "time is money and quality is an even greater commodity." When I bid on a job, I am very specific in what it is that I am going to deliver and I deliver it on time. I try to deliver early to give the client the opportunity to review the work and ask for any changes they may want to make.

If there is a problem, one that I feel the client needs to be involved in to fix, I let them know immediately¾and I don't beat around the bush with it¾in order to have everything I need to address the issue so I am not taking up their valuable time, or mine for that matter. I try to have a few options prepared for resolving the issue before I talk to the client, then let them choose which option that they prefer.

Communication is huge for a freelancer. It can be a little scary for a client, not having the ability to "drop in" and check on how the work is coming along. Recently I have started utilizing a platform called "Trillian" as a means of communication. It is great for the quick communication, touching-base, or passing along a bit of information. I actually prefer it to emails. It is a more extensive form of IM.

9. Do you have any tips on how to effectively manage your time?

Time management is another big part of freelancing. If you lack time management skills, it will be difficult to be a successful freelancer.

There are no supervisors to watch over you and no time clocks to punch. It is ALL on you to manage your time and your workload.

I have a calendar that sits right next to me at my desk. I also utilize alert systems and a daily planner (online & hard copy). I set up an alarm system that alerts me every two hours so I can monitor my progress... and it reminds me to get up and stretch.

Before I begin a project, I gather all of the tools that I will require in order to accomplish the task. This way I don't waste time starting and stopping because I am missing something. Everything I need is within my reach or a roll of my chair.

When I bid for the job, part of that process is determining how long the job would take. I always block extra time for every job... just in case. As much as I would like to control every aspect of my day that will never happen. So I prepare for the unexpected.

10. Do you prefer working by yourself or is freelancing a lonely life?

The answer to that question is, a little of both. I worked in the health care field for many years and developed a sort of "selective hearing." It was the only way to block out the unnecessary noise, but my instincts were always fine-tuned to hear an emergent situation or recognize when it was time to pay attention to the activities of the team.

There are certainly times I miss the hustle and bustle of the brick and mortar job routine. Granted, I have quite a fewer interruptions in my working environment, but it can also get very quiet... almost a little too quiet. That's when I take a break and revisit the real world.

11. Do you have any other tips for people who want to be successful freelancers?

Very few people become successful over night. It takes patience, fortitude, and stubbornness to become successful as a freelancer.

- If you really want to break away from the conventional work place, start your freelancing career now, while you still have a job

- If you are out of work, try to find part-time work to supplement your income until you build up your freelance business

- Put together a professional portfolio that serves as an example of your work

- Network! Join LinkedIn and other organizations

- For Writers and Editors, join affiliated groups such as NAIWE

- Develop a Website

- Get PAID! If you are working through a freelance website, don't start the job until it has been funded

- Get a Contract! If you are not working through a freelance website, be sure you get a signed Independent Contract Agreement and part of the payment up front. I prefer receiving my payments through PayPal

- Take personal time, go visit a friend, take the dog for a walk, something... but don't spend all of your time working, alone

- Take good care of yourself, exercise, eat properly, drink lots of water or you will discover how quickly the pounds can add up

Cathy Reed

www.cathyreedediting.com

1. What do you enjoy about being a freelancer?

I enjoy:

- setting my own hours
- the huge variety of the work and the clientele; I find it fascinating
- working with clients in dozens of countries (so far, I have had clients in 46 countries)
- learning so much about so many different subjects – things I didn't even know existed
- the fact that it's portable and you can do it anywhere
- the excitement of never knowing what's coming next, or who you're going to be working for

2. What don't you enjoy about being a freelancer?

No benefits (medical, dental, etc.)

3. Would you advise a friend to become a freelancer or would you advise they get a normal 9 to 5 job? And why?

Over 7 or 8 semesters I taught a course at a local college: "The Business of Online Writing & Editing".

It was extremely popular, especially with retired government workers, managers, and teachers, and also with students who had just graduated. It was always full to capacity. I also gave presentations to writer's groups, etc. However, I realized over time that a huge percentage of people get discouraged very easily because it's highly competitive field and it takes time to build up a business.

So I would say that you really need to have the entrepreneurial spirit and drive. And part of that is being excited about the unknown and the possibilities.

4. What do you think is the best freelancing site and why?

The only one that I've found useful is Elance.

- Because they are actively engaged in keeping up with the times and making their site the best it can be.
- And because they attract great clients from all over the world, businesses, professionals, good writers. (Lots of not-great clients too, but it's easy to weed out the good ones.)
- Also, Elance has a great search engine; so if you're an active provider, you'll pop up when clients use the search engine.

5. Have you ever picked up work outside of the freelance sites and if so how did you find this work?

Some people find me on LinkedIn, so it's important to keep your LinkedIn site current and active.

Many people who find me on Elance or LinkedIn also check out my website, so it's important to have a professional website.

I also get some work through my local editing association.

And I get some work from local universities, especially Profs who are working with PhD candidates, but also other Profs and students.

6. Do you have any tips on how to win freelance jobs? (either on the freelance sites or outside of these).

- On Elance (or other freelance bid sites): Create very specific bids and include with each bid a couple of relevant samples and some relevant testimonials.

- Create folders (on your computer) where you can quickly grab samples or testimonials for different types of jobs.

- If the subject is an area where you have particular experience or expertise or interest, say so. That is often important to clients.

- Be enthusiastic!

7. Do you have any tips on how to accumulate good feedback on the freelance sites?

- First of all, don't bid on a project that doesn't really suit your area of expertise. Bid on projects where you know you can deliver a great result.

- Always check out the client's profile (easy to do). If it's a client that has posted 8 jobs, only hired for 3, and not bothered to give feedback or given poor feedback – this is the client you don't want. If it's a professional client that has posted 8 jobs, chosen good providers, and then given them top marks – that's the type of client you want.

- Always do a *great* job for the project, not just a good job.

- Sometimes there's an opportunity to provide something extra. For example, if you're editing a manuscript, you can offer the name of a talented (and not expensive) cover designer.

- Be enthusiastic about your work and about helping the client in whatever he/she is trying to do.

- Deliver ahead of schedule. Clients love that.

8. How do you keep your clients happy?

- I do a great job and often go the extra mile, whatever that means for a particular project.

- If I can, I deliver ahead of schedule.

- My work is mostly manuscript editing. To better serve my clients, I have a list of talented (and fairly priced) cover designers and book/ebook book layout professionals that I can refer my clients to. I also have a list of indexers and translators.

9. Do you have any tips on how to effectively manage your time?

On a weekly basis, and for a number of weeks, keep track of the amount of time you are working that is billable hours, and the amount of time that is non-billable hours. Once you have a realistic picture, ask yourself if you're satisfied with that.

Also, from that picture, decide if there are some things you can do to cut down on the non-billable hours. For example, can you make templates or keep files of certain types of bids or certain types of work.

10. Do you prefer working by yourself or is freelancing a lonely life?

I don't find it lonely at all. I turn on my music and dive into the manuscript/project.

I belong to an editing association and I have coffee sometimes with editors or writers or graphic designers or clients. It's fun to compare notes.

11. Do you have any other tips for people who want to be successful freelancers?

- I'm not a huge social networker myself, but there are endless writing and editing blogs and LinkedIn groups, etc. that you can check out.

- Also, it takes time. If you open a new coffee shop in a town that's full of coffee shops, you won't have hundreds of clients the first day. You'll need to get creative and think of lots of ways to market yourself and spread the word.

- Ask yourself if you have the entrepreneurial spirit. If you don't, you'll get discouraged with the time and effort it takes to build your business.

Chris (Clarity Translations)

www.translationsbyclarity.com

1. What do you enjoy about being a freelancer?

I particularly enjoy being able to decide how much time I am going to dedicate to each aspect of my life. Although I usually spend quite a few hours working each day, I know I can take a break now and then to dedicate myself to other activities, like going to the gym or having a coffee with a friend, while still meeting my deadlines. I also have the chance to work from anywhere with an access to Internet: I can enjoy my favourite Frozen Cappuccino at the local café and work on a project at the same time. I can go for a quick trip to the nearby countryside and finish an assignment right before going for a walk in the meadows.

2. What don't you enjoy about being a freelancer?

Being a freelancer can be lonely sometimes, especially if you are working by yourself, as opposed to being part of a company. The lack of immediate feedback from a colleague can be discouraging sometimes. If you are working on several projects at the same time, it may mean less free time during weekends, or long working hours. In this case, it is up to you to take measures so you don't get 'burned out'.

3. Would you advise a friend to become a freelancer or would you advise they get a normal 9 to 5 job? And why?

I am always telling my friends and family about the advantages of becoming a freelancer. Although a normal 9 to 5 job offers certain stability, it also puts a glass ceiling over your head in most cases. Being a freelancer means making decisions for yourself, from which jobs you want to work on, to how much you want to earn, and how much you want to work. I always hear them complain about their normal jobs, either because they are bored, they don't earn enough money, or they have a less than satisfying relationship with their bosses and workmates. Another aspect I highlight when I encourage them to develop a skill that can lead them to become freelancers is the freedom you get from working anywhere and at any time. You don't have to be chained to your desk for 8 hours a day, you can go out and work from the part if you want to.

4. What do you think is the best freelancing site and why?

In my area of expertise, I would recommend joining Elance and Proz, because they are reliable, they have plenty of job postings and a robust profile system that allows you to showcase your abilities and background in a clear way that brings you more business.

5. Have you ever picked up work outside of the freelance sites and if so how did you find this work?

My primary source of jobs are the freelance sites I mentioned above, but sometimes I get jobs from referrals, and local colleagues who need a hand with the projects they have been awarded. In the case of referrals, it is often useful to ask a satisfied client to recommend you to his or her colleagues whenever they need translation services.

6. Do you have any tips on how to win freelance jobs? (either on the freelance sites or outside of these).

Communication is key. Clients often feel uncertain about the quality of work or the results they will obtain, and communicating often and clearly can help minimize fears on the client's side. Having a great portfolio is also essential, with lots of examples of previous jobs. If you are new and haven't got any experience, it is a good idea to simply show what you can do, even if it means taking a short paragraph of a well-known novel and translate it into the target language. It might be easier for designers who usually have a portfolio of art to show to potential clients. It is also important to specify the scope of your service, how much time it will take you to complete the task, and what the fee includes.

7. Do you have any tips on how to accumulate good feedback on the freelance sites?

Happy clients help you accumulate good feedback and win referrals. If you communicate often, meet deadlines, and charge a reasonable fee, it is very likely that the client will leave a good review. Sometimes, problems may arise within the project, and it is important to go the extra mile to solve it in a way that the client will be satisfied. Be polite and mind your grammar, regardless of your area of work. Be available and make sure the client has more than one way to contact you. Show interest and be grateful once the project is complete. In short, think of how you like to be treated when you hire somebody or go into a store to buy something, and emulate that positive behaviour. You may also need to be ready to accept you have made a mistake, and offer ways to compensate your client. All of these details will help you get good feedback.

8. How do you keep your clients happy?

As I mentioned before, in order to keep clients happy you need to communicate often and clearly. At the beginning, it is important to understand exactly what the client wants. If they are looking for fast turnaround, you will be better off providing a strict deadline that you can meet within the time available. Make sure you know exactly what is expected; ask any questions beforehand. Show professionalism: be polite and speak/write properly. Let them know as you make progress when they can expect to receive an update, especially in long-term jobs. Be grateful for the opportunities they give you and offer to provide your services again in the future. In certain jobs, it may be useful to offer further assistance. For example, one of my clients was travelling to Spain right after I sent him the translated document he had assigned to me, and I offered some quick Spanish lessons that he could read while on the plane, free of charge. He was really grateful and continued to send me jobs whenever he needed translation services.

9. Do you have any tips on how to effectively manage your time?

Time management is really tricky. There are a number of books and resources to learn how to manage your time that suggest making to-do lists, track your progress and set a timer. I particularly use lists and a timer, and I usually try to make progress on the most demanding tasks during the morning. You need to know when you are at the peak of your energy during the day, and use that time to work on the most challenging tasks. There may be a lot of distractions, like online magazines or websites that will drain your energy and waste your time, and you need to avoid them whilst you are working. It is useful to set daily goals in order to make sure you will meet deadlines and not fall behind.

10. Do you prefer working by yourself or is freelancing a lonely life?

Working as a freelancer can be lonely sometimes. The lack of a second set of eyes or another brain to help you think can be discouraging, but there are a few tools you can use to overcome this, such as forums for specialists or the use of Skype to chat with a colleague to find a solution or get their advice. I prefer working by myself because it gives me freedom to make my own decisions.

11. Do you have any other tips for people who want to be successful freelancers?

If you are interested in a career as a freelancer, you may need to develop a lot of skills in addition to the ones you will offer as a service. For example, you will need to have many roles within your business, as you have to sell your service, be your own boss in terms of discipline, and even be your own accountant. Don't expect immediate results, it may take you some time to find your first client. It is important to start slow, and keep your day job for a little longer before relying completely on your income as a freelancer. You will have to keep up to date in terms of technology, websites offering tools for translators and so on. Being a freelancer can be demanding sometimes, and if you tend to be lazy, this may not be the right path for you. A freelance career involves being proactive to make your business thrive. And I always recommend placing the concept of providing a great service at the top of your priorities, even before earning an income.

Vladan Filipovic

https://www.elance.com/s/edit/ficoman86/

1. What do you enjoy about being a freelancer?

Well, in the first place it is free time I have. I can easily organize myself, my time and easily manage my obligations. I always know up front what my tasks are and after I'm done, I always have time for other activities. This work gives me an opportunity to manage my own life and to achieve a balance between work and all other things that make life great. You also meet a lot of different people all around the globe, learn a lot about their countries, share different thoughts and experiences. It is also great that you can learn a lot and upgrade your knowledge. I have done a lot of jobs and each one was different from another. This is because I love to work on different projects which gives me an opportunity to learn new things and develop my way of thinking.

2. What don't you enjoy about being a freelancer?

There are only a few things that I do not enjoy, but they are not so important. First, it is sometimes hard to sit in front of the computer for a whole day and you have to take a walk from time to time. Second, it is not always a 100% stable job. Its stability depends on clients. There are times when there is just no job for you; you want to work, you need money, but there are no good clients or there is just no demand for your services. Perhaps this is the most important reason; the uncertain nature of this work.

3. Would you advise a friend to become a freelancer or would you advise they get a normal 9 to 5 job? And why?

In my case I do both jobs. I have a regular job and I work as a freelancer. I would advise a friend to become a freelancer, mainly because of the reasons I enjoy being a freelancer: you manage your life and your time, you can always plan few steps ahead, there is no boss to look over you, if you do not feel like working, you can just stand up and take a walk, you gain a control over your life¾you are not just some kind of a marionette. These are all things that are not always included in normal job (except if you work for Government like I do, but still there exists a pressure from the other side). I had to start working as a freelancer, because I could not earn enough for living with my regular job and I would advise anyone who has this kind of issue to follow my steps. Doing a freelancing jobs gives you an opportunity to do some interesting and creative work that you can't do in your regular, 9 to 5 job. You can also learn a lot and you have time to find a best way on how to perform magnificent work, which is almost impossible in a regualar job, when you lack the time.

4. What do you think is the best freelancing site and why?

In my opinion it is Elance. Their site looks perfect, you have a lot of options for interacting with your clients, it has a high accessibility and it is user friendly. Another thing which is very important is a level of professionalism from their support stuff. They just stunned me! They will always listen to your opinion and help you achieve your rights as a freelancer. The payment system also works perfect.

5. Have you ever picked up work outside of the freelance sites and if so how did you find this work?

No. I always tend to work with eligible clients and I'm just not interested in that kind of work. You can encounter a lot of fraudsters out there.

6. Do you have any tips on how to win freelance jobs? (either on the freelance sites or outside of these).

Work, work and work! One word which is so important. If you want to earn more money and to be respectful freelancer, you will just have to roll up your sleeves and get to work. When you get the first job, you just have to devote yourself 100% to do it right. If you just want to earn money without hard work, it is better you do not start this freelancing adventure.

7. Do you have any tips on how to accumulate good feedback on the freelance sites?

As I mentioned above TO WORK HARD is the best tip. Also, it is very important to always satisfy your clients' needs. Once you receive your first feedback it will mark your entire career as a freelancer, so the first feedback is the most important thing you can get. Like the first mark in your school: if you get and A they will always think that you deserve an A and will restrain themselves to give you an F. FIRST IMPRESSON is key.

8. How do you keep your clients happy?

By satisfying their needs. It is just very simple. Client is always right, because he is the one who gives money and expects a good favour in return. Do you want to pay for something which you do not like? Or do you want to pay for the service which is under you expectations? You must sometimes go beyond your borders and walk and extra mile. Everyone likes being served and treated as a king. Do you? One more thing, it is also very important to be professional and friendly at the same time. You must find a balance between these two things¾sometimes you encounter a clients which only wants a professional relationship and sometimes you encounter a clients which wants a friendly and personal relation. Psychology is also very involved in this matter. You must think deep and WORK HARD.

9. Do you have any tips on how to effectively manage your time?

Always plan 10 steps ahead. Think on long-, not short-terms. Focus yourself on the goals, not on the measures for achieving it. Take a piece of paper and make a plan. Whatever you write on that piece of paper, just do it. Avoid thinking; it is not impossible, it is unreal and other negatives. Always be positive and be sure to respect the things you write. My emphasis is on writing, because when you write something it stays there, when you type something on your computer you can just delete it, as if it has never happened. Paper brings magic and makes your plans come true.

10. Do you prefer working by yourself or is freelancing a lonely life?

For now, I work alone. In future, maybe I'll expand my services and find another partner. This is always an option. Freelancing is definitely not a lonely life. You always encounter different people and characters. I was amazed about many different personalities I met during my work. Most of them were good and honest people. They also share the same passion and desire to be successful like you do.

11. Do you have any other tips for people who want to be successful freelancers?

I will be boring, but I must say it again; work hard, be professional and friendly and respect clients' needs, especially their money and time. There is a reason why you've been picked for the job, so it is up to you to justify yourself. I have a phrase which best describes this: "The harder I work, the luckier I get", which means the more quality you incorporate into your job, the better results you will achieve; more client satisfaction, which leads to more jobs and which leads to more money earned.

Mel @ Quality Admin Solutions

www.qualityadminsolutions.com

1. What do you enjoy about being a freelancer?

Being able to freelance is a tremendous privilege. One is able to work from home and enjoy a certain degree of independence and flexibility. I got my first freelancing gig via Elance in 2009. One project led to another. My client testimonials and project history on Elance raised my profile which enabled me to be more selective with projects I choose to work on. Fast forward to today, I remain consistently ranked in the top 100 Elance freelancers out of 177,021 admin support services providers globally. I now have a loyal client-base providing a steady income stream. It just goes to show that hard work and determination do pay off.

Outlined below are reasons why I derive huge satisfaction from being a freelancer providing admin support services to clients on Elance.

FLEXIBLE WORK HOURS & WORKPLACE - BEING THE BOSS – WHAT DO I WANT TO DO TODAY?

Life is all about choices, right? No more fixed working schedule and goodbye to Monday-itis. If you're the type who prefers to work afternoons and into the evening – yes, you can. Don't want to work this Friday? No problem – take the day off!

I set my own hours i.e. I can now work anytime during the day or night and my commute is within seconds - from my bed to my computer/work station. My choice of work outfit – my call!

My work station set-up – no more do's and don't's. And, I can be mobile meaning I could be working from any part of the world and it's business as usual.

The take-away message for me here is; better job satisfaction and productivity which translates to a win-win situation for both customer and freelancer.

BUILDS SELF-ESTEEM.

Stats don't lie. Since joining Elance in 2009, I've maintained my ranking in the top 100 best performing admin freelancers (approximately 177,021 Elancers) in the world, along with the top spot in Australia.

I thrive on repeat business from loyal clients. It's a testament to my good work and my win-win relationship with my valued customers.

To date, I enjoy relative success as a freelancer on Elance. I attribute it all to my hard work, perseverance, my decisions and efforts. Credit is all mine.

FREEDOM FROM NOT HAVING TO DEAL WITH OFFICE POLITICS.

Every workplace has one and more so with large organizations. I've worked in both public and private sectors. When it's vicious and personal, it's almost unethical. I found that being neutral is not an option as it can affect your work-social networking environment. Plus, I'm really not cut out for it. So, this is definitely one of the pros of being in business for yourself. The upside - no more annoying co-workers and/or distracting work situations.

CONTROL - WHO'S IN CHARGE?

I alone decide which projects I will purse and accept. No more oh-great-ones breathing down my neck or bosses to drive me nuts! The best part is not having to explain why I'm doing things the way I am. Totally in-charge, I have a say in everything most specifically, deadlines. I'm my own boss. Cool.

2. What don't you enjoy about being a freelancer?

As they say, there are two sides to every story. Based on my experience, here are some of the negative aspects of freelancing. If there was no downside, I bet everyone would be doing it! But I can confirm that the pros definitely outweigh the cons of freelancing, so much so, that I'm quite happy to put up with the downsides.

Financial Security/Uncertainty

It's true, freedom comes with a price. It may be that I'm extremely busy one month and the next month may just be the opposite. Fact is - if I don't work, I don't get paid. How hard I work will determine how much I make.

Freelancing can be something of a double-edged sword. So, when I decided to become my own boss, I gave up the following:

- regular salary
- paid time off (days off / sick / vacation leave)
- employer superannuation payments
- work-provided gadgets
- office resources i.e. latest office technology
- permanent / long-term employment

Stiff Competition

Some buyers who hire freelancers honestly believe they should not have to pay much. Freelancers tend to be overworked and underpaid. This is due to the fact that competition is very tough factoring in the cost of living in certain countries. It holds especially true with online platforms like Elance, where some freelancers from all over the world are prepared to offer the same services for less than half of what you can offer the client. Thankfully, in my case, my good work record and client testimonials have tremendously helped in getting those gigs where clients are prepared to pay extra for quality.

PAYMENT DISPUTE

I have a conflict-averse personality so online-staffing platform like Elance suits me to a T. Having a work environment where NO face-to-face interaction with the client exists - is simply awesome.

Unfortunately for me, since I joined Elance in 2009, I've had two or three clients who never paid for the work I had delivered. The client suddenly disappeared, never to be heard from again. After three or four courteous reminders to no avail, I stopped chasing.

Then, there's the new customer or repeat customer who will leverage the Elance feedback mechanism even if you've delivered great results for them. They'll use it as a bargaining tool for the next project. I feel this is tantamount to the client passive-aggressive bullying the freelancer. Just my two cents.

Unfortunately, there are unscrupulous buyers who are out to take advantage of unsuspecting freelancers either by paying them a substandard rate, not paying on time or withholding payment, etc.

Having stated all of the above, believe it or not, I'm still learning to this day how to recognize valuable and non-valuable buyers.

ONE-MAN BAND

I have to wear many hats and/or be a jack of all trades to be able to manage my business. I've stopped counting the number of projects/ offers I've declined to date because I'm unable to accommodate them all. I once hired another freelancer on Elance who I thought would be an ideal person to help with my overflow work. The job was basic, straight-forward data entry in MS Excel. Despite clear instructions provided and constant contact, it turned out that quality and accuracy were not the main focus but rather turnaround. I ended up re-doing the work myself. Sub-contracting did not work for me.

After that negative experience on Elance, I never hired an extra pair of hands again. Grow my business? I think small is the new 'big' and small works just fine for me. Staying solo allows me to ensure the quality of my work is maintained to client's satisfaction. Happy clients, happy me!

WORKPLACE SOCIAL EVENTS

Yes, I'm definitely missing out on Friday night's get-togethers, long & lazy lunches, Christmas parties and what have you. No biggie!

3. Would you advise a friend to become a freelancer or would you advise they get a normal 9 to 5 job? And why?

I'd most likely recommend freelancing to a friend who is a full-time, stay-at-home mum looking to earn some extra cash. If she has the knowledge or education and set-up at home to be able to offer freelance services in areas which she is especially talented – why not. This would be an excellent choice for her.

Obviously, for those who have to provide for their families i.e. private school for the kids, mortgage, credit card payments, lifestyle, etc. a 9 to 5 job would be a much better and more intelligent option. A permanent, long-term relationship with a single employer translates to financial security. There's no argument there.

4. What do you think is the best freelancing site and why?

Elance – no contest there! I also signed up with oDesk around the same time in 2009. It's the other major player in the freelance industry. After winning back to back projects on Elance, I ended up cancelling my membership with oDesk as Elance kept me busy enough.

BTW - I learned recently that Elance & oDesk have merged albeit still functioning as separate platforms. Best wishes to both of them.

5. Have you ever picked up work outside of the freelance sites and if so how did you find this work?

Yes, through my own personal website (www.qualityadminsolutions. com) which exclusively caters for non–Elance clientele.

I'm cognizant of the fact that having the Elance widget to showcase my client testimonials on my website definitely helps in boosting my website/profile as a reliable provider of admin support services. A huge thanks to Elance for this free marketing tool. Elance rocks!!!!

6. Do you have any tips on how to win freelance jobs? (either on the freelance sites or outside of these).

CLIENT TESTIMONIALS

Having good performance reviews, no doubt, can help persuade prospective to consider working with you. Therefore, they'll want to know what projects you've been involved in, who else you've worked with and what your interactions with other customers have been like. They'll want to know if you are reliable/credible or not.

It also gives the prospective buyer an overview of your work strengths, dcmeanour/attitude, and what you're looking for in your next project. What's the best form of advertising? Yep, a good plug from happy and satisfied customers. Client testimonials very much come into play when the buyer makes a hiring decision. That's why client satisfaction is so crucial to freelancing success.

Let your good work speak for you – enough said!

REPEAT CUSTOMERS

It's the foundation of successful businesses, big or small. Repeat business or customer retention can easily convert to client referrals.

Sometimes, satisfied clients don't want the fuss of having to start again with a new freelancer anymore than the freelancer wants to lose a good buyer.

Therefore, it is critical to commit to quality not just quantity i.e. the more value you offer, the more a client will depend on you. Create client trust by keeping your promises and try to go the extra mile whenever you can. When a repeat client asks me for a certain number of quality business leads, I always endeavour to deliver more than what was requested (think conversion rate). It's a token of goodwill i.e. I'm reciprocating my client's investment in me.

WORK PROFILE.

Raise/build your profile by highlighting your talents and proven skills via showcasing your online test results, etc. If possible, make your CV brief and to the point. Your profile should work for you while you are busy working. Also, put on display general samples of work you've done for other clients (subject to client's approval) to see; and observe confidentiality and discretion as you see fit. The latter has put me in good stead with my clients to this day.

MANAGE CLIENT'S EXPECTATIONS.

- Submit tenders only for projects that you are certain you can perform (and perform very well – be honest from get go).

- If you've been invited to bid for a project and you think you're not the right fit, decline it respectfully. Do not ignore the invite as the client will take note of it.

- Communication is a 2-way street. Try and understand the clients' requirements prior to submitting your bid. Don't hesitate to ask questions if you feel something does not make sense. Client will view this as your eagerness to work with them. And, when you do hear from the client, respond to their message promptly and politely.

- Under-promise, over-deliver. It's better not to promise something to your customer that you can't deliver. If you deliver what you've promised and more, from then on client trust and satisfaction grows.

7. Do you have any tips on how to accumulate good feedback on the freelance sites?

Feedback needs to be earned. Establish a track record one client at a time.

Generally, happy customers have no hesitancy leaving a good review for a freelancer. In cases where you've identified these happy customers and they did not leave a feedback for you, it may be because of time constraints or they simply don't know how to go about it, etc. You may need to reach out to them and ask if they'll do a review for you to help you garner similar calibre of clients.

"YOU WILL BE JUDGED BY WHAT YOU DO, NOT WHAT YOU SAY."

For me, it's all about consistency and making absolutely sure my customers are happy. When I tackle my client's projects, my main focus is how to get good results/outcome for them. My clients may not be aware of the fact that I do always throw in something extra – it could be delivering way before the promised date or putting in the extra hours, free of charge, just to make sure the quality of my work does not suffer.

8. How do you keep your clients happy?

Becoming the consummate professional, always deliver quality results, clear communication and superb customer service.

I consistently provide excellent service to my customers. I anticipate their needs even before they even know their own requirements. I deal with them in a respectful manner at all times. And, I normally put in extra hours, at no cost to my clients, to ensure that I've done my very best to achieve an ideal outcome for them.

9. Do you have any tips on how to effectively manage your time?

- Set work/life boundaries. Communicate to your family and friends your schedule and obligations as a freelancer. Your work station is a work station, just like a proper office. Most importantly, make sure they fully know and understand that when you are working – you are working!

- Set a schedule and stick to it. Keep your schedule consistent and don't make it a habit to work longer hours than you have to.

- Don't over-commit yourself. Learn to say NO without feeling guilty lest the quality of your work suffers. Remember, if you get sick, there's no one else to cover for you.

- Continue to plan your holidays and let your regular clients know your away dates well in advance. They will thank you for your initiative and cooperation.

- Avoid burnout and look after yourself. Focus on diet, nutrition, exercise, relaxation and de-stressing.

10. Do you prefer working by yourself or is freelancing a lonely life?

Autonomy is a major attraction of freelancing. I thrive in autonomous roles even when I was working in large organizations. I've a natural aptitude for it. When you are accountable for your decisions, you are happier and more productive in your job. Solitude suits me just fine. I work best alone.

11. Do you have any other tips for people who want to be successful freelancers?

Freelancing is not for the faint-hearted. It does not suit everyone. Despite the ultimate freedom and flexibility it offers, you've no-one else to blame when things go wrong. So, for those who have chosen it and are serious about it, here are some tips for successful freelancing:

- Focus on providing an excellent service every time – think long-term results.
- Look after your regular clients – they are your walking billboards.
- Time management – be super organized and practice discipline.
- Skills evaluation – keeping your skills current will keep you in demand.
- Patience and determination – there's no time to rest on your laurels in the freelance world.
- Independence costs money. The uncertainty of freelancing i.e. unstable income can be a killer. Therefore, plan your finances wisely and manage your cash-flow. Create a budget and seek professional help if you need to. Have an emergency fund to pay bills. Split your bank accounts i.e. one for personal savings and one for operating your business. Curtail spending on unnecessary items and save, save, save.
- Always do the right thing – no matter what!!!

Solange Basseterre

linkedin.com/in/solangebass/

1. What do you enjoy about being a freelancer?

One of the things I enjoy the most is the possibility of working on many different projects. Each client is different as are his working and communication styles, so each new project is a completely different experience from the previous one. Of course as you gain more experience, you perceive better what to expect, but it is still a new experience. The entire cycle begins from zero, the introduction, negotiation, coming to understand your client's expectations and so on. I've worked with clients from all around the globe, and with other freelancers too, from the United States, Israel, Netherlands and many more; and I find it truly fascinating to experience the cultural differences. One project can have the client in the United Arab Emirates, the Project Manager in Argentina, the designer in the US and the developers in Pakistan; all coming from different cultures and in different time zones, so I really enjoy working for all those pieces to come together and form a functional team.

I also believe working as a freelancer drives me to stay updated on the latest tools and tendencies, forcing me to keep learning and improving myself. As a freelancer nothing can be taken for granted, so if you get too comfortable you can eventually become obsolete. You need to keep in mind how competitive the market can be. You are not only competing with local talent, you are competing with the entire world; it is a healthy and wonderful competition but in the end that's what it is: a competition. So far I've loved every step of it; I've learnt more in the last couple of years that what I learnt in all my years working on a regular job.

And last but not least, of course I love having flexible hours. This can be a tricky concept, I know, since having no set working hours means that you end up working at all hours, especially when working with clients with a time difference of over 5 hours. But as time pass and you learn how to organize your work, you learn how to avoid ending up working on a Sunday at 9 PM because you don't want to miss a deadline. You will always have the advantage of being able to choose whether you want to work until late at night and sleep more, or the other way around. You can take your time to go to the bank, the doctor, or anything else without having to ask for anyone's authorization. In my personal case just not having to travel downtown to an office saves me more than 4 hours a day, which I can use to sleep a little more in the morning or to spend more time at home in the evenings.

2. What don't you enjoy about being a freelancer?

I'm not sure there is anything I don't enjoy, but the thing I enjoy the least is the income instability. Although I do very well, I earn more money than having a full time job; I still need to be very careful when projecting each month's income. Sometimes you project to collect on a job in February and an unexpected delay comes up and you know you won't collect until March, so you need to check whether you have enough money or if you will need to land another quick job to cover for that.

But this is another aspect that you easily improve with some experience. As an advice for new freelancers, what is important is not to get carried away and trust that what you made for two months will be what you will always make, they need to be cautious. It's important to keep clean records so you can compare projections to actual collected payments and eventually learn your business rhythm.

Another aspect I don't enjoy much is that, besides my experience, after delivering certain jobs I still get nervous about the client not liking the results. I'm a perfectionist; so many times I have that sensation that it could have done better and that makes me a little anxious. So far every client has been more than happy with the results, but if any freelancer reading this finds himself in the same situation, I would like to say: Don't worry; it happens to many of us. And although it is a good thing to trust in your own talent and relax, it's also good not to get too comfortable and risk becoming reckless.

3. Would you advise a friend to become a freelancer or would you advise they get a normal 9 to 5 job? And why?

That will depend 100 % on my friend's personality and skills. Having a regular 9 to 5 job is not for everyone; well, it is the same about freelancing.

When you are working on your own, and it is your intention to only work as a freelancer with no other source of income; then you become all areas of a company. You are accounting, administration, marketing, PR … all of them. So no matter what your skills are or your talent is, if you are a terrible communicator you will eventually be in trouble.

You need to be a highly proactive person, you have no supervisor or anyone around to tell you that you are working too slowly or that you have wasted enough time for one day. A freelancer has to be very organized and self disciplined. But most importantly, a freelancer needs to have a lot of self criticism. This is not only the most important factor but the most difficult one.

If you are the kind of person who always assume the reason why another person won a job is because he/she was cheaper (sometime it's true but not always), or that the only one with a problem is the client, and you have a hard time writing a list of your flaws and weaknesses, then this is not the right business for you. You need to learn from other freelancers and know how to appreciate in which aspects are they better; you also need to learn where you failed in a chain of communication. Even if a client is difficult, was there any better strategy to reach him? Did I just make his confusion worst?

Relationships are everything in this business. For example a designer might think that all that matters is the final design, but he also knows how important the communication process is in order to understand client's needs. And if you ever encounter any delays or problems, which could happen to anyone, the relationship will be all that matters. It makes a huge difference. If you have a client that feels that you care and he is comfortable within the project, any potential problems will reach him differently than if he is uncertain of the results or already annoyed about the communication process.

So if you feel you are not a good communicator, negotiator or that customer service is not your strength then I would advise you team up with someone that is. You can also take some courses, but what is important is not to underestimate the importance of the commercial aspect of the freelancing business.

4. What do you think is the best freelancing site and why?

I would have to say Elance. It has a wide variety of working categories and it's the one that makes the biggest effort to maintain a certain standard of work. As every platform it attracts all type of clients, but even if within a certain category the average hourly rate is of USD 11, you can get work for USD 30 an hour. You just need to find your niche.

For me it is very important what type of clients a platform attracts. A client wants the best freelancers, well, we want the best clients. Every platform becomes an ecosystem. So even the communication style on job post can become contagious, and if I go into a platform and I have to read 50 posts in which they are underestimating freelancers, the tone is patronizing and offers are almost ridiculous, then I have nothing to do there.

I provide a very professional service and do my best to always exceed expectations, so I intend to be treated as a professional. And I feel very comfortable within Elance.

Then there are other good platforms, but they are too focused on other areas. So the variety of posts is not enough for me. But this will depend on each freelancer's area of expertise.

5. Have you ever picked up work outside of the freelance sites and if so how did you find this work?

Yes, I have. It was always because of "mouth to mouth". If I don't know the client or I have no reference then I like to suggest taking the contract to a platform.

But so far, all clients that have reached out to me outside of a platform were people who knew me from old jobs or who were referred to me by another client or freelancer.

I don't discard having a personal website some day and attract clients that way, but so far I haven't had the need, so maybe in the future.

6. Do you have any tips on how to win freelance jobs? (either on the freelance sites or outside of these).

In my experience, in order to win a freelancer job you need to be able to answer the question: why should the client choose you over the other freelancers?

The answer might seem easy, but it is not. You need to determine your competitive advantage. If you are only cheap, you are giving up on quality. And if you are one of the most expensive then you can't trust that the price speaks for itself. "Expensive" does not equal "Quality"; you will have to eventually address the cost-benefit relationship.

A freelancer needs to keep in mind that a client will probably review many proposals; and that part of what you are saying is been said by other 20 freelancers. So, why you? In certain areas a portfolio helps a lot, but what if a client is indecisive between a few proposals? Then other aspects of the "service" might be what make up his mind.

My advice is to take a piece of paper, in one column write all the reasons why a client should hire you and on the other one all the reasons why a client might choose another freelancer. You need to know your weaknesses so you can balance your proposals. That list will give you the aspects you need to address in your proposals and a more clear idea on how to address them.

I have seen many freelancers who write vague proposals and suggest a call to discuss the projects. Most clients don't have time to talk to all the freelancers who suggests the same and they don't want to risk their time by ending up talking to a freelancer they know nothing about. So even if this is your strategy make sure you are giving them a good reason why they should make time to talk to you; have ready some very good bait.

7. Do you have any tips on how to accumulate good feedback on the freelance sites?

I follow two standards: quality and honesty. Make sure everything you do is high quality from your first communication to the final delivery.

Always start your communications with a Thank You note, be respectful. A freelancer can have some flexibility with his communication style, as long as he remembers he is not chatting with a friend. Always use proper grammar and keep in mind you don't know the person on the other side or what his/her "style" is, so try to stand in the middle.

And above all be honest. If you are not sure whether you will be able to deliver something on time, or you have doubts whether the information the client wants is available, just very professionally address these issues, clients value this every time. If you have to communicate something negative or you need to say "no" to a client, you need to be very subtle and be sure you explain the reasons without offending the other person or starting an unnecessary argument.

Nobody likes excuses, nor the freelancer or the client. So make sure you accept jobs that you know you will be able to deliver on time and that are 100% within your area of expertise. Your reputation is everything you have.

And above all, don't ask for good feedback. Don't make the feedback become a part of the package, they are already paying you for your job. You don't work for feedback, you work for money. So don't make feedback become part of a bargain. 90 % of my clients leave feedback without me having to ask for it. If they appreciate your work they will take the time, and if not, it will give you a good reason to analyse the process and its results.

8. How do you keep your clients happy?

I never over promise and I make sure every time they read a communication from me they can imagine a smile in my face.

It is not the client's fault if I'm swamped, tired or if there is a storm outside. They trusted me with a job. If possible, over deliver and let them know how much you appreciate their business.

Deliver on time (earlier if possible), on budget and with a smile on your face.

9. Do you have any tips on how to effectively manage your time?

In the beginning everything is chaos. You do all estimates wrong: budget and delivery dates. So coming up with a schedule is almost impossible.

But later it is important to decide from what time you will get up every morning to what time will you have lunch. If you are handling multiple projects allocate a specific amount of time to each. If you just improvise you will find out that something you estimated would take an hour took three so now you don't have enough time for another pending project. So make sure you have a daily schedule, if something gets delayed you can take a look at the schedule and modify it, but at least you won't realize you forgot something once it's too late.

One of the best ways to manage your time is by not trusting your own memory. Trying to remember very simple tasks can become very distracting. So I recommend using any Project Management or Task Management software so you can upload and keep track of tasks. It's an Action-Action system; any action leads to another action until the project is over. If you have just sent an email to a client and you cross that task out, you open another task as a reminder to check if you received the answer. This will help your mind relax and you will become more efficient.

10. Do you prefer working by yourself or is freelancing a lonely life?

Both. I love freelancing and I wouldn't change it for anything. But I miss certain aspects of being part of a team; a local team not a virtual team. Sometimes I feel like a lion in a cage.

But there are many things you can do to balance that. You can work some hours on a co-working space or in a coffee shop. I don't do it for many reasons, I use more than one monitor, I get distracted, etc. But in my case I decided to go back to the university and enrolled on a post graduate program. So at least twice a week I go to the university and share with new people and I also have the opportunity to work as a team. So if you work at home it is very important not to live in your pajamas; get dressed every morning, do your makeup and hair (well, I'm a woman after all) and also try to find some activities besides your work.

11. Do you have any other tips for people who want to be successful freelancers?

Be humble. Learn from others, from yourself and from every experience. Be grateful for what you have and for the fact that you have the opportunity of being a freelancer. Be generous with your clients, with other team members and with other freelancers. All of this eventually pays off and you will have a blast.

Stacey McLennan

www.copycatservices.com

1. What do you enjoy about being a freelancer?

COLLABORATING WITH PEOPLE WORLDWIDE. As a Canadian, I have had the opportunity to work with people globally. I have engaged with clients from the United States, the United Kingdom, Ireland, and Australia. It is truly an incredibly rewarding experience to provide services for individuals and businesses around the world.

ESTABLISHING LONG-TERM PROFESSIONAL RELATIONSHIPS. I thrive off of serving my clients with superior service and referral-worthy results, and building a high number of loyal clientele. Building a business and generating revenue. By investing my time, dedication, and hard work to guarantee exceptional service and top-quality output to consumers, this also develops my business' success by securing long-term clients and increasing profits.

TIME FLEXIBILITY. Family is fundamental in my life. My family is my motivation and drives me to succeed. I am a stay-at-home mother of two young children, a 1-year-old and a 2½-year-old, and it is extremely important that we can spend quality time together. I sincerely appreciate that I can be at home as an influential mother and that I have the freedom to take them to weekly gym classes and special events.

2. What don't you enjoy about being a freelancer?

Time flexibility does not mean time freedom. Sometimes sacrificing sleep by staying up late and getting up super early is required to keep on top of everything. Freelance work and building an online business does not have a punch-in and punch-out time; I work during the day, evenings, nights, and weekends. By having a smartphone always on-hand – every email, notification, and phone call that comes in no matter what time of day – I'm on high-alert. I love being busy and the work that I do, but find it extremely difficult to "un-plug" or have "time off."

3. Would you advise a friend to become a freelancer or would you advise they get a normal 9 to 5 job? And why?

To begin with, I would suggest both. Secure a 9 to 5 job while establishing yourself as a freelancer. This way, you will have a steady revenue stream. When you are a new freelancer without regular repeat clients and without projects on the go – there is no guarantee you will be bringing in money. As you build up your online presence, loyal clients, and reputation, you will come to a stage in your freelance career where you can leave your "9 to 5" and provide online services on a full-time basis.

4. What do you think is the best freelancing site and why?

I personally prefer Elance. In comparison to other sites, I find it easy-to-use, reliable, and there are plenty of new jobs posted daily. The majority of my clients today are from Elance.

5. Have you ever picked up work outside of the freelance sites and if so how did you find this work?

- I have received a number of jobs by posting my services on free online classified ads.
- I recently launched a website, www.copycatservices.com, and use Google AdWords to drive traffic to the site.
- I registered my services, phone number, and website with search engines and multiple online people/business directories.
- I have also received clients through word-of-mouth referrals.

6. Do you have any tips on how to win freelance jobs? (either on the freelance sites or outside of these).

Building your reputation is paramount. As a beginner, it may help to take a price cut for the first few jobs to get yourself out there, obtain relevant experience, and to accumulate positive feedback. There is a lot of competition online, so you have to establish a profile so that you stand out from the crowd.

The proposal you submit (job application) is also very important. By writing a professional and unique proposal, you will get noticed. Incorporate the prospective client's job details in your bid so that they recognize you have carefully read and fully understand the particular job requirements. Be sure to include your distinctive talents, why they should hire you, and what you have to offer that will contribute to their project's success.

7. Do you have any tips on how to accumulate good feedback on the freelance sites?

Be communicative, responsive, and put your client first! You need to provide all-around excellent service. You must be professional throughout all interactions. Start off by thanking the client for choosing your services. Be accommodating – find out what the client wants, get the job specs, and deliver! Do not cut corners, and treat your client exceptionally well.

Give your client an update on your progress to ensure that everything is running smoothly with the project. If you happen to come across any issues, be sure to communicate your concerns promptly. Make sure that the deadline you commit to, you will deliver on. If the project is time-sensitive, it is reassuring for the client to receive an update that the work is in-progress and on schedule, and that you will deliver on-time – if not, sooner.

When you have completed the job, ask the client if there is anything they want changed or done differently. Again, be accommodating. From my experience, you do an outstanding job and there will rarely be anything to change. When you have received confirmation that you have fulfilled the client's expectations, show appreciation by saying: "Thank you for the opportunity to work with you."

8. How do you keep your clients happy?

- By being communicative, responsive, and readily available.

- Always following through on commitments.

- By valuing and enjoying engagements with each and every client as an individual.

- Crystal clear clarity: by finding out what the client wants, precisely how they want it, and when they want it by – and then delivering service correspondingly.

- Investing time, effort, and hard work on all projects whether big or small, and continually providing optimal service.

- By genuinely caring for the client and their project, and never-failing to accentuate that in the final deliverable.

9. Do you have any tips on how to effectively manage your time?

As a stay-at-home mother of two young children not yet in school – I work around their schedule. I stay up late, wake up early, work during their nap, and work in the evening.

10. Do you prefer working by yourself or is freelancing a lonely life?

I work equally well with others as I do independently, but do not find freelancing a lonely life, as I interact with multiple people daily either by phone or email.

11. Do you have any other tips for people who want to be successful freelancers?

Get in the game. Create a profile, work on your proposal, and start putting bids out there. If you are working full-time, there are many projects that do not require a speedy turnaround time.

Make sure you are pursuing a career that you are passionate about. Freelancing entirely revolves around self-motivation, so you need to find something that you enjoy. If you dislike what you do, it will be easy to lose interest and burn out.

Be persistent and persevere. If you are not awarded jobs right away, try not to get discouraged and do not give up. Keep on applying for jobs, tweaking your proposals, and improving your profile.

Devika Joglekar

http://www.miheika.com

1. What do you enjoy about being a freelancer?

FREEDOM

I have freedom to work on the projects I like and I can say *no* to the projects I don't like. I can decide my hourly rate. Since I am not designated to a particular title like an illustrator or animator, I can work on variety of projects like animations, children's book illustrations, cover art, graphic design, lettering, etc. Also, I get a chance to work with people from around the world.

FLEXIBILITY

I can work on my own schedule and it gives me the liberty to pursue my hobbies. Also helps that I don't need to commute in rush hours and bad weather! I can go on a vacation whenever I want.
Couldn't ask for more. :)

2. What don't you enjoy about being a freelancer?

ISOLATION

I miss the socialization that happens at the job place.

INSECURITY.

Freelancers don't have a steady stream of income. Consequently, I always have to be alert of how many projects I need in order to meet my financial goals.

3. Would you advise a friend to become a freelancer or would you advise they get a normal 9 to 5 job? And why?

YES.

Freelancing allows you to live your life on your own terms. If you have courage to fight with the uncertainties and you are passionate about the work you want to do, then why not?

4. What do you think is the best freelancing site and why?

ELANCE.

I have been using it for the last 5 years. It has really good job postings in Design and multimedia category. Most importantly, Elance Escrow has payment protection for freelancers.

5. Have you ever picked up work outside of the freelance sites and if so how did you find this work?

YES.

Networking always helps. If you are good at what you do, people always recommend you. I ran a comic strip in a newspaper for 4 years. It provided exposure for my work and established me as an artist.

Also, it opened up doors to many publishing houses.

6. Do you have any tips on how to win freelance jobs? (Either on the freelance sites or outside of these).

PORTFOLIO

Art is the field where a strong portfolio and good feedback win jobs.

There are always great jobs available. You need to be vigilant and aggressive enough to win the job.

Networking

It is crucial to win new opportunities.

If you provide quality work on time, most of the time, clients have new jobs for you in the pipeline and they give you good feedback and recommendations.

7. Do you have any tips on how to accumulate good feedback on the freelance sites?

Do an awesome job!

You can always ask for a feedback. If the clients get the desired work done well, they are happy to give you a good recommendation.

8. How do you keep your clients happy?

If you are working with a new client, he/she is as apprehensive as you are.

Quality work, correspondence and on time delivery are the three key things that make the client happy. It also increases the chances to get a steady workflow from the same client.

9. Do you have any tips on how to effectively manage your time?

Whilst working I keep away from distractions like Facebook and Twitter. An uninterrupted workday is a productive workday.

Every day, I allot separate time for work and for marketing.

10. Do you prefer working by yourself or is freelancing a lonely life?

Sometimes, it feels lonely. But, I can focus better on my work.

I love to do what I want and how I want. I think that's important.

11. Do you have any other tips for people who want to be successful freelancers?

- Stick to your expertise and make a good portfolio.
- Set goals.
- *Network* with people in your field.
- Never undervalue your work.
- Work on the projects you are really interested in.
- Give your 100% and deliver on time.
- Learn new tools.
- Be brave and embark on your project right away. Remember, well begun is half done!

Laura Russell

www.adminkitty.com

1. What do you enjoy about being a freelancer?

I started freelancing in June 2013 as a part-time job to earn some extra money and to fill in some available time on the weekends. As I was growing my business, I found several reasons why I have been enjoying the life of a freelancer:

    ∞   I can set my own hours. As a person who works a full-time job as well as freelancing on a part-time basis, I am enjoying freelancing because it has allows me to work when I want to work. If I want to stop work in order to spend some time with my family, I can. If I want to work until 2:00 AM in my pajamas, I can. I like being my own boss and working when it is convenient for me. The time I spend pursuing this portion of my career is directly connected to my own personal goals for success.

    ∞   I choose who I want to work with. Through Elance, which is the only freelance website that I utilize as part of my business, I have the ability to look at feedback that clients have received from other freelancers. Looking at client's feedback is a good indicator on whether a client is good to work with, or difficult. If, after my client research, I find that they have good feedback, then I am more comfortable bidding on their projects. Freelancing has its risks: there are clients who will take a freelancer's work and then not pay for it, or want a hundred revisions without paying for the additional time … but the savvy freelancer can negotiate and avoid some of those obstacles through research and being diligent.

    ∞   All jobs are not the same. Freelancing allows me to be creative and perform work that is not routine through my day job. I provide administrative, word processing, formatting, and document services. I truly enjoy working with a variety of businesses, meeting a variety of individuals from around the world, learning more about their company and their industry, and I normally learn one new skill on every project that I work on.

∞   I am motivated to increase MY business. Freelancing is a bit of a game to me; how can I inform the client that my services are better than my competitors? Can I write a better proposal than my competitor? Can I provide better samples to sway the client that I can best suit their needs? How much more money could I make this week than I made last week? Competition and motivation is what drives me to succeed at my business.

2. What don't you enjoy about being a freelancer?

There are only a few issues that I do not enjoy about freelancing.

∞   Payment and other financial matters. With Elance, when I am awarded a project, the client funds an escrow account, so I know that the money is there, waiting until I complete a project, then those funds are released to me. For direct channel clients (who arrive through adminkitty.com), that escrow protection is not there. It has been difficult for me to determine how to best invoice clients and I worry that I will not be paid because I do not have that escrow account for a guarantee of payment. What if I complete a project and the client does not pay me? What if, even if I provide them an estimate up front, they end up saying that it is too much? Once, I provided an estimate to a company in Australia for $600 and they agreed to those terms. When I invoiced the company, they paid me in Australian currency and not in U.S. currency, which was about $150.00 less than my invoice. I had no clue how to handle that, and the company refused to fund the currency conversion. I took it as a learning opportunity, and I now make sure that clients who come through my website understand that I expect payment in the form of U.S. currency. For larger scale projects, I take partial payments throughout the project (while furnishing what work has been completed). This way, neither side is adversely affected.

    ∞   Freelancing takes a great deal of time away from family, especially if you also work a full-time job. I wake up at 4:30 AM, get ready for work, and while I am waiting for my husband to get ready for work (we carpool together), I spend time either working on my freelance projects, contacting clients, or looking for other projects to bid on. I spend break times during the day contacting clients or looking for new projects. When I get home from work at 5:30 PM, I check client messages, have dinner and spend an hour or two with my family, and then I freelance until 9:00 or 10:00 PM. I tend to work all days on Saturday and Sundays, driving my business. This can cut into other routines and responsibilities, and if you live with others - development of that support is critical. Success takes hard work, commitment, and time.

3. Would you advise a friend to become a freelancer or would you advise they get a normal 9 to 5 job? And why?

At this point in my business, I would not advise anyone to quit their day job to freelance on a full-time basis. It takes time to grow your business, to forge relationships with clients, who hopefully, will turn into return and repeat clients, and the competition is fierce. I have found, through persistence, intense time, and focus that I am able to return a clear income benefit- but not all people may find such success initially. Test the waters, test yourself. Prove your commitment and intensity in a real way before burning any bridges that might be tethering you to security. My ultimate goal is to freelance on a full-time basis, but I am afraid that I would not be able to consistently bring in the money that I need to make, and I do like having the benefits that my full-time job provides (medical insurance, 6 weeks of vacation, etc.). If you are unemployed, or underemployed, and have significant skills- then by all means pursue it with vigour.

Bear in mind the realities: I have offered the "hows" and "whys" of getting into the same opportunity that I have - but have found that not all people have the same level of commitment, and are more comfortable working for others than for themselves. Freelancing is not a get rich quick scheme, it is not a way of avoiding hard work - it is a field of opportunity in the new millennium, and rewards diligence, hard work, and perseverance.

4. What do you think is the best freelancing site and why?

When I started looking into freelancing, I joined several sites, including oDesk and Freelancer.com, but I ultimately signed up with Elance (as a paying member) because I found the site to have a more professional level of clientele and it is where I found my first freelancing gig, which makes it more special than other sites. With Elance, I like that there is a large assortment of projects listed, I like that there is escrow protection, and their customer service support is top notch.

5. Have you ever picked up work outside of the freelance sites and if so how did you find this work?

Since I started freelancing, I have created my own website (www.adminkitty.com) and have developed (through the help of another Elancer) a professional Facebook and LinkedIn business account. So I am also growing my business through my website and LinkedIn. In my field, your reputation is a powerful marketing tool - and I am fortunate to now have clients seek me through these alternative sites.

6. Do you have any tips on how to win freelance jobs? (either on the freelance sites or outside of these).

To be successful on freelancing sites, you have to be hungry for the work. I am constantly scanning projects as they become available. When I go to the bathroom, I have my phone in hand looking for projects to bid on: I reply to all client invitations to bid on their projects. New projects are being listed all the time and you have to stay on top of it. You also have to spend quite a bit of time writing proposals – as this may be your only shot at presenting who you are to a prospective client. When I was looking for someone to help me create my Facebook and LinkedIn business accounts, I put out a request to freelancers who perform this type of work. Some of the responses were horrible, and it was obvious that some individuals did not bother reading what I was asking for. I even had freelancers who would just send me a one line response that said "Hire me". I spend a great deal of time on the proposals that I submit to clients. I address why I feel I am the best match for their project, I list all of the skills I have that they need for their project to be successful; I propose a plan of action of how I would approach their project, and I provide relevant samples. While I do not get all jobs, the ones I am awarded are at the compensation levels I feel are commensurate with my expertise.

7. Do you have any tips on how to accumulate good feedback on the freelance sites?

Communication! I have found that clients are hungry for communication. They want to know what is going on with their projects. They like having questions asked because it makes them feel as they are a part of the projects. All of the feedback that I have received has something about what a great communicator I have been.

Time management. Do not over commit, but meet the commitments

THE CROWDSOURCED GUIDE TO FREELANCING

you make. The classic adage "under promise and over deliver" works equally as well in the virtual world as in the brick and mortar marketplace.

8. How do you keep your clients happy?

I am myself with my clients. I am friendly, I will make suggestions on what might better their project, I stay in constant contact with my clients (I provide at least one update per day), and I am always on budget, and their projects are completed either early or by the deadline. I am also firm and fair if I must either decline an additional request, or if I feel that the project is going beyond the scope and expectation set by the client prior to the bid.

9. Do you have any tips on how to effectively manage your time?

I do not have time management problems when working on one project. However, when I have three or four projects going on at the same time, and getting requests for proposals from other clients, it can be a bit frazzling. When I have more than one client, I tend to set aside a certain amount of time per day on their project, then I spend a certain amount of time on the next project. Most of the projects that I work on have a 1 to 3 day turnaround time. My biggest tip is; learn how to utilize time more effectively and how to prioritise work.

10. Do you prefer working by yourself or is freelancing a lonely life?

I have always been a lone wolf and prefer to work by myself. I have tried hiring another person to help me when I had too many projects to do myself, and found myself disappointed. When it is your name and brand on the line, it is often easier to manage the project yourself. It is far from lonely, however - I have made friendships and connections with clients - and the nature of some projects ensure that my email inbox is rarely empty. I am fortunate to have a family to spend time with when I want in-person companionship. I would suggest that anyone seeking to pursue freelancing, to schedule time volunteering, or seeking others to incorporate some socialization into their weekly routine.

11. Do you have any other tips for people who want to be successful freelancers?

Again, if you want to be successful at freelancing, you have to take it seriously and you have to be 'hungry'. You have to dedicate a lot of hours and money into building your brand, having the correct and up-to-date tools, your clientele, your portfolio, and your reputation (your feedback). You may also wish to pursue something you are already an expert in, or have a sincere interest in. Believe in yourself, and study how the system works.

Tatiana Wiedemann

Main Language Pair: English <-> Portuguese
tatiana.wiedemann@gmail.com

1. What do you enjoy about being a freelancer?

What I enjoy most about being a Freelancer is the flexibility it allows me to have regarding my working hours and the place I work at. Even though any Freelancer has to be extremely disciplined in order to get all of their work done and of course, on time, I can still make my own schedule, work any time I want and where I want—all I need is my laptop.

2. What don't you enjoy about being a freelancer?

What really puts me down as a Freelancer is that some clients don´t have respect for my job. Being a Freelancer is like having any other paying job. Some clients don't see this, they sometimes expects us to work for free in order to get "your name" on the market. From my point of view, that is really disrespectful as you wouldn´t treat any other professional this way.

3. Would you advise a friend to become a freelancer or would you advise they get a normal 9 to 5 job? And why?

That really depends on a few things. If that friend was comfortable with not having a steady paycheck and was extremely disciplined, then yes. But, if that friend needs a paycheck every 5th of the month, or has no self-discipline whatsoever then being a Freelancer is not the right choice.

4. What do you think is the best freelancing site and why?

I really like using Elance.com, but that is just because I am already used to the platform. oDesk is good too. But you don´t need to depend on websites all the time. As long as you have a good portfolio, you can always gain clients without having to be linked to a certain site.

5. Have you ever picked up work outside of the freelance sites and if so how did you find this work?

Yes. Build a great portfolio and don´t be afraid to "sell" your work by sending as many e-mails as you can to prospective clients.

6. Do you have any tips on how to win freelance jobs? (either on the freelance sites or outside of these).

Starting out as a Freelancer is no piece of cake as you compete with many people who have much more experience than you. When I first started, I got my first job by being completely honest about being a new freelancer; I guess I was lucky that the client liked my honesty and my portfolio. My suggestions is, build a great portfolio, set reasonable fees and hope you get a client that has faith in you. We all start off somewhere.

7. Do you have any tips on how to accumulate good feedback on the freelance sites?

From my experience, to get a good feedback from clients, do a great job. Clients like to see that you have put some extra effort and consideration into their project.

8. How do you keep your clients happy?

Never, ever, ever miss a deadline. For me, deadlines are sacred. Once you miss a deadline, even if it is only by a few hours or a day, most likely you will have also lost a client.

9. Do you have any tips on how to effectively manage your time/

My time management is pretty straight forward. With every new project I take, I estimate how many days it will take me to get it done. Once you know how much work you have to do in order to deliver the job on time, work till you meet your daily goal, no matter if it takes 2 or 10 hours.

10. Do you prefer working by yourself or is freelancing a lonely life?

Freelancing definitely is a lonely professional life. However, it does have its upside of not having anyone telling you what to do. So, for me, it counterbalances the loneliness.

11. Do you have any other tips for people who want to be successful freelancers?

Be positive, the start of a new career is never easy and don´t give up. We all had our first chance of showing our work.

Emma Brown

www.elance.com/s/kaorixi/

1. What do you enjoy about being a freelancer?

I enjoy the flexibility and the freedom of being able to work at my own pace and during any time; day or night. Working from home also affords many advantages, not having to commute and being able to be a Mum who, although working hard is at home for her children.

2. What don't you enjoy about being a freelancer?

The biggest downside of being a freelancer is the uncertainty whether you will have enough work coming in often enough, also tight deadlines when family life takes up more time than one can afford resulting in many nights spent working until the small hours.

3. Would you advise a friend to become a freelancer or would you advise they get a normal 9 to 5 job and why?

If somebody needed to work with the flexibility and freedom that freelancing allows, then of course I would recommend it. However, the earnings can be very low when bidding for work along with other freelancers around the world. When a freelancer in India is bidding, they can offer much lower rates then we can in the UK, so if you need to have high earnings, I would recommend a 9 to 5 job.

4. What do you think is the best freelancing site and why?

I have only used Elance so have no opinion on other sites, but I am kept fully employed through this site alone.

5. Have you ever picked up work outside of the freelance sites and if so, how did you find this work?

I haven't picked up work outside of any freelance site as I have no spare time available.

6. Do you have any tips on how to win freelance jobs?

The only way to ensure you win freelance jobs is having the best reputation but to get this, your work must be accurate and always on time. Don't miss your deadlines!

7. Do you have any tips on how to accumulate good feedback on the freelance sites?

Always ensure you deliver fast and accurately. Always have good communication and let the client know if you are having difficulties; they will generally understand as long as you are clear and honest.

8. How do you keep you clients happy?

I always deliver what has been asked for and try to deliver before the deadline. Always check your work and ensure it is accurate.

9. Do you have any tips on how to effectively manage your time?

I always put in the hardest hours at the beginning of the contract so that I am not up against such a tight deadline. If you have a lot of time to get a project complete, don't leave it until the last minute, sooner rather than later always works best. Ensure you always allocate certain 'working hours' and stick to them. Treat your day as if you have gone into the office to do your work, no exceptions.

10. Do you prefer working by yourself or is freelancing a lonely life?

For some it could be lonely, but for me it is perfect. I can socialise in my free time, but working alone means I am very productive.

11. Do you have any other tips for people who want to be successful freelancers?

Be willing to work hard and go the extra mile. Putting in many hours can result in some great outcomes when trying to win clients. The world is not always on your time zone so be willing to work at night as well as during the day.

www.ingramcontent.com/pod-product-compliance
Lightning Source LLC
Chambersburg PA
CBHW051723170526
45167CB00002B/770